A SHORT HISTORY OF RELIGION IN AMERICA

A Short History of Religion in America

Lester B. Scherer
Eastern Michigan University

Advocate Publishing Group
6810 East Main Street, Reynoldsburg, Ohio 43068

For Ruth and Dessa

My other mothers

Cover design by J. Howard Noel

ISBN: 0-89894-011-7

10 9 8 7 6 5 4 3 2 1

Printed in the United States of America

CONTENTS

ACKNOWLEDGMENT

No work of general scope can claim to rest primarily on the author's original research. My research experience is represented in parts of Chapters Three and Four. The bulk of the information and much of the interpretation in this book depend on published articles, studies, and general accounts. The bibliography is intended in part to show something of the pattern of my dependence. Some of these publications are cited in the chapters by author and page number in parentheses. It will be evident in some instances that my debt to particular authors goes beyond the specific citations.

CHAPTER ONE

Religion In American Life

Religion has a special place in American life. Observers from other countries have for many years commented that religion is more important here than in other western countries. One British writer called the United States "the nation with the soul of a church". Whether we agree with him or not, the fact is that America has a more varied and active religious life than most other lands. Even in this age of secularization a high percentage of Americans are religiously active.

The Nature of Religion

Religion is the pursuit of salvation. "Salvation" means

different things to different people, but it always carries the idea of overcoming life's worst problems and gaining life's highest satisfactions. The following list suggests the major threats to our well-being.

- pain
- crippling injury or illness
- loss of livelihood
- shame and guilt
- mental turmoil or disorientation
- sorrow or depression
- death of important person in our lives
- rejection by important persons
- fear of any of the above
- fear of death

"Salvation" in any religion means avoiding or overcoming these threats and moving instead toward the following goals.

- health and strength
- triumph over suffering
- adequate livelihood
- dignity and self-respect
- serenity
- joy
- supportive relationships
- feeling of harmony with the universe and its ruling powers
- triumph over death

The idea of salvation seems to be at the heart of all religion. No religious community can endure unless its adherents believe they are involved in a process that protects them and leads them to fulfillment. Life being what it is, religious people must suffer hardship, but they feel that without the resources of religion they would be much worse off.

Religion, then, consists of the things that people do in their quest for salvation. Religious activity can be conveniently divided into four categories: beliefs, ritual, obligations, and group interactions. Religious *beliefs* are convictions about what is real and what is good; for instance, "God created the world out of nothing" or "It is wrong to work on the Sabbath" or "People are more valuable than things" or "I have lived many previous lives." Taken together, a person's beliefs make up his or her "world view," or basic attitude toward self, others, the world, and the future.

Ritual consists of symbolic words and actions by which people relate to what they believe is extraordinarily good or powerful (for instance "God" in the Jewish and Christian religions). Some ritual acts are lengthy and complex, such as the High Mass. Others are as simple as bowing one's head. Some rituals have been standardized with written instructions. Others have grown out of spontaneous acts and are not even recognized as ritual by those who do them; for instance, the often repeated gestures and phrases of a Pentecostal prayer meeting. Some people think of ritual as useless and boring, and of course there are some dry, empty rituals. But there are also rituals that are alive with relevance and power for the people who take part in them. In fact people often find their deepest joy or sharpest insights during rituals.

Obligations are the patterns of behavior that people undertake because of their beliefs: the acts we "ought" or "ought not" to do. The most demanding religious obligations are those that regulate one's behavior toward other people. These are sometimes stated very broadly, as "Love your neighbor as yourself." Sometimes they are specific, for example telling how to calculate what you should pay to someone you have accidentally injured.

Under *group interaction* we include all occasions when members of a religious group gather for any purpose. The pursuit of one's salvation usually requires the support of other people performing several functions: consoling, explaining, celebrating, listening, advising, encouraging, resolving conflict, and other behavior that relieves suffering and promotes well-being. It is fashionable these days to speak of religion as a private and solitary matter, but effective religions are seldom practiced alone. People need people, and religion provides the most accessible structure for serious, helpful interaction.

The Religious Identification of Americans

The most obvious feature of religion in this country is its variety. The most complete listing of American religious bodies (Melton 1977) includes 1,275 "primary religious groups," while omitting others for technical and pragmatic reasons. Granted that some of the groups listed have only a few hundred adherents, the variety is enormous, not only in the number of groups but in their types: Southern Baptists and flying saucer religions, Roman Catholics and Black Jews, the Native American Church and the Greek Orthodox Church.

Furthermore, religious affiliations vary by region. In the South there was a saying, "If you're not a Baptist or a Methodist, someone's been tampering with your religion." In some counties in the Southwest and the

Northeast, Catholic affiliation runs 80 or 90 percent of those who do have a religious affiliation. Similarly Utah is Mormon country (Church of Jesus Christ of Latter Day Saints). There are lighter but still impressive concentrations of Lutherans in the upper Midwest and of Jews in New York and certain other metropolitan areas. Even small groups have a tendency to bunch up and alter the religious culture in certain localities, as with the Mennonites in parts of Indiana and Ohio and the Dutch-derived Reformed groups in parts of Michigan and Iowa. So it is hard to find a location from which to view the spectrum of America's religions.

One way to gain perspective on the national population is to imagine one hundred "typical" Americans, eighteen and older, answering certain questions. "Do you believe in God or a universal spirit?" Ninety-four will say Yes, and about the same number are willing to state a 'religious preference' (more about this below). However, only seventy-one of them will say they are *members* of a church or synagogue, that is, actually claim a religious "affiliation." Now ask the same hundred people, "Did you yourself attend a church or synagogue service in the last seven days?" and about 42 of them will say yes. This question has to be asked in a typical week, not during summer, when attendance is low, nor the week after Easter, when Christian attendance soars for one Sunday. Compared to the 10 and 20 percent attendance figures for the European countries, Americans show a strong commitment to weekly worship.

Taking the affiliation and attendance figures, is it possible to use them as indicators of religious interest and then to go one step farther and make historical comparisons? Many Americans believe that "people are less religious" compared to some earlier time, while others claim that we are "experiencing a great spiritual revival." It is hard to confirm or refute such impressions with the data we have, yet the figures do suggest some sort of comparison. It is often estimated that religious affiliation just after the Revolution was no more than 15 percent of the total population (not just the adult population, as with the figures above). Religious affiliation increased through the years to a peak of 64 percent of the total population in 1965. Then the percentage declined somewhat during the following decade before showing a slight recovery in the late seventies. The figure now stands somewhere around 60 percent. No one claims that these figures indicate that Americans are four times more "religious" now than they were two centuries ago. For one thing the membership requirements of the main Protestant bodies were much stricter then, so that many adherents or "constituents" were not actually members. Nevertheless the figures do indicate the strong religious interest of Americans today.

Surveys of religious attendance among persons eighteen and older are available only for certain years since 1939. These figures vary from a low of 36 percent in 1942 to a high of 49 percent in 1955 and 1958. After 1958 the figures steadily declined, leveling off at 40 percent from 1971 through 1975. There has been a slight increase since then. Attendance figures vary according to locality and group. Catholics attend at a rate of about 55 percent (down from 71 percent in the 1960s), Protestants 40 percent, and Jews 20 percent. Comparing these figures with religious attendance before 1939 is a matter of careful guessing. There is no way to learn how many people attended a house of worship during the week of George Washington's inauguration. However, there is no reason to suppose that Americans as a whole ever surpassed the 49 percent figure recorded in the 1950s. In fact it is likely that religious interest has remained at about the same level throughout our history. Therefore present-day announcements of religious ruin or renewal should be viewed with caution and carefully examined to see what facts they are supposed to be based on.

Turning back to our hundred typical Americans, it will be remembered that all but a few of them are willing to state a religious preference. This is helpful because it gives the student a view of a broad pattern emerging from among the thousand-plus religious bodies in this country. Using survey information from the middle 1970s, we discover that ninety percent of the hundred express a preference for some form of Christianity, as follows:

Protestant	60
Roman Catholic	27
Eastern Orthodox	2
Other Christian	1

Of the ten remaining out of one hundred, three state that they are Jews, making Judaism the largest non-Christian religion in the United States. Two persons state that they prefer some religion other than Christianity or Judaism. Represented here are such classic world religions as Islam, Buddhism, and Hinduism, as well as Native American religions and many other groups, some originating in this country and some with overseas backgrounds.

The last five persons in the typical hundred state that they have no religion. They may mean exactly that, or they may mean that their religion is strictly private, with no name or group. Sociologist Thomas Luckmann introduced the term "invisible religion" to refer to this phenomenon. Religious freedom in this country includes the freedom to have no religion or to make up one's own religion. Television and radio, books and magazines, memories and conversations: these together offer endless resources for assembling private religious beliefs and practices. Of course this is not a new thing, nor is it limited to those who declare they have no religion. Many Catholics, for instance, have private beliefs and practices that are not consistent with Catholic teaching. The same observation applies to any organized religion in a modern society. But invisible religion, the entirely private and unorganized variety, may have increased in the last twenty-five years and may be increasing now. Looking at the figure we started with, the number of people who say "no religion" increased from 3 percent in the middle fifties to 5 percent in the late seventies. It is not clear how to interpret that change, but it will be interesting to keep an eye on that figure in the years ahead.

Organizing A Short History

The variety of religious traditions in the United States, along with the multitude of developments through the years, challenges the writer of a brief religious history. This book consists of descriptions of the major streams of religious practice. This plan has the advantage of producing maximum clarity in a short space. Time references within the chapters, together with the chronological lists at the ends of the chapters, will help the reader understand how the separate traditions were related to each other at different times.

One way to imagine the religious development of the American people is to picture a land in which traditions have been added layer on layer. Beginning with the earliest tradition, then, we look first at the Indians (Chapter Two). Although Catholics were the first Europeans to colonize parts of North America, later events placed British Protestants in control of the territory from which the political history of the United States began. Therefore Chapter Three deals with European-derived Protestantism. When the United States became independent in 1776, one out of every five persons was African by birth or descent. Most of them were enslaved. These people created a religion attuned to the conditions of slavery and racial oppression (Chapter Four). Catholics were a rare species in the British colonies, but later conditions sent millions of them fleeing from Europe to the United States, resulting in the largest religious organization in this country (Chapter Five). At the same time, special dangers directed at European Jews brought many of them to America also (Chapter Six).

It seems to me that any attempt in this context to produce a final summary chapter and opinion is likely to result in repetition and empty phrases. Therefore the reader will discover that the book stops but does not really end. It is hoped that concise historical description will prove valuable in itself as one of many approaches to understanding religion in the United States.

CHAPTER TWO

Indian Religion: America's First Faith

We often speak of the United States as a nation of immigrants. We are of course mostly descended from Europeans who chose to cross the Atlantic or from Africans who came as captives. Yet our history books frequently read as if these people came to an empty continent, which, of course, is not true. There were a million or so North Americans here when the first European explorer stepped ashore. Because of the error of an explorer, these first Americans were called "Indians," a name that today is accepted by Native Americans as a useful label to refer to all pre-Europeans on this continent, together with their descendants.

If we look far enough into the past, we find that the first Americans were immigrants too. They were Asians who probably began arriving in North America more than 20,000 years ago. There was once a great land bridge where Siberia is now separated from Alaska by the Arctic Ocean and the Bering Sea, sometimes as much as a thousand miles wide, called the Bering Platform. In the course of thousands of years, people migrated across it, gradually moving eastward and southward all over North and South

America. At the end of the last Ice Age, around 8000 B.C., the Bering Platform was flooded by the water from melting glaciers, and the continents were separated. Further immigration took place by water, but the bulk of the prehistoric Indian population had already arrived. As the centuries passed, these people intertwined the patterns of living brought from the Old World with patterns discovered and perfected on this continent.

Indian Culture

One misconception about Indian life is that it has been always and everywhere the same. For most white people, the controlling image is the one presented for many years in films: feather bonnets, horses, and buffalo. Actually that horse-centered culture dominated only one part of the continent and flourished only during the nineteenth century. Indians did not even have horses until shortly before 1700.

The variety of Indian life-styles is suggested by the fact that in pre-European times they spoke 500 to 1000 different languages and dialects. Evidence reported by archeologists and anthropologists shows that Indian cultures not only differed from each other but also changed greatly with the passing of time. Clans and tribes merged or split or migrated. New environments demanded new skills, new patterns of cooperation, and new religions. People devised countless ways to obtain and prepare food, to protect and adorn their bodies, and to construct shelters.

A convenient classification of Indian cultures is the simple division between hunter-gatherers and planters. Hunter-gatherers are those who exploit the environment just as they find it, gathering plants and animals for food and fiber. The prosperity of such a culture depends on the generosity of the environment, for no amount of skill can gather what is not already there. For instance, the desert basin between the Rockies and the Sierras presented a constant challenge to survival and could support only a sparse human population. Yet each season presented certain edible plants and small animals by which life could be sustained on a more or less predictable basis. Tribes such as the Utes built an austere but dignified culture in that inhospitable territory. By contrast, the hunter-gatherers of the eastern woodlands enjoyed an environment much richer in water, plants, and animals, supplying the people with an ample, varied diet and a less rigorous life. The

Indians of the northwest coast, timber cutters and hunters of sea mammals, are another example of a prosperous culture based on hunting and gathering.

The beginning of agriculture was a great turning point in the history of humans in general and of North American Indians in particular. Methods of growing food instead of merely gathering it arrived late in North America. Having arisen in central America perhaps 7,000 years ago (3,000 years or so after originating in Western Asia), agriculture slowly spread northward. Although there are signs of corn-growing in the Southwest and the lower Mississippi Valley beginning about 2,000 years ago, it did not become important until around 500 A.D. By the time the first European explorers arrived in the sixteenth century, planting was spread unevenly as far north as the Great Lakes. Corn, beans, and squash were the main food crops, while in some places cotton was grown for fiber and tobacco for ceremonial incense.

By stabilizing the food supply, making it more predictable and more localized, agriculture transformed Indian life in several regions. Planters could abandon seasonal food-gathering migrations and establish permanent villages and towns. Some of these were physically impressive, such as the huge apartment house communities in the Southwest, and the Aztec-like plazas and temple pyramids of the lower Mississippi. In general, planter communities could support more people in a smaller space, in some cases towns of 1,500 or more. They also tended to develop stricter social divisions, sometimes with hereditary royalty and nobility at the top and the commoners below. In religion, the planters developed some features that hunter-gatherers did not have, such as permanent temples, separate priesthoods, and prolonged public ceremonies.

One of the interesting developments of Indian history occurred when some planting tribes first migrated to the Great Plains. During the century in which white colonists in the East were moving toward revolution, these Indians were acquiring horses. Reversing the usual pattern of development, they gave up agriculture in favor of a life based on buffalo hunting.

Each pattern of culture included a corresponding pattern of religion. When the culture changed — in connection with a changed environment or a new method of getting food — important features of the religion would also change. Among agricultural people, the most important religious ceremonies are tied to the growth cycle of major crops, while big-game hunters center their ritual on seasonal hunts. People who live in small groups in tough environments, where survival depends on constant cooperation, are likely to emphasize the ritual of group membership, such as those connected with birth and initiation. In some groups, the religious emphasis is on acquiring individual power, while in others the main concern is to avert collective disasters. The different environments also provide different sacred objects and personalities: ocean or sun, eagle or bear, mountain or river. The variations and combinations are endless.

As we consider major features common to all Indian culture, it is important to remember that Indian religion is not dead, because Indians are not dead. Despite a disastrous encounter with white American culture, there are about as many Indians in the United States today as there were within the same area when white people first came here. Many of them continue the lively traditions of their ancestors. As we shall see, Indian religion is still adapting to new needs and new circumstances, just as it has done for thousands of years.

The Indian World View

In these days of concern about our environment, many non-Indian Americans have become aware that Indians traditionally have had a different view of the relation between people and the natural world than that of white culture. For a long time, white people have looked upon human beings as the only beings worthy of consideration. Religious teachings stated that God made the world for people. Animals and plants, though technically alive, are available for exploitation without any consideration except the welfare of human beings. Apart from humans, animals, and plants, everything on earth is inanimate, "dead," and likewise may be used in any way that people desire. Jewish and Christian religions encourage this attitude, categorizing the whole non-human world as "resources." The only question they require us to ask is: "Are we using God's gifts wisely?" Dams, factories, and oil wells are among the many monuments to this point of view; unparallelled (and unequal) material wealth is its most dramatic and evident social result.

The Indian point of view is different. Virtually everything in the Indian's world is alive and requires some form of consideration. Human beings are important, but they must approach every feature of the world as if it too has life and power. Animals are especially prominent in this scheme, and Indians typically regard them as kinsmen and great spirits. But trees and food plants, and even the grass one walks on, are alive and must be related to rather than simply taken. Beyond the biologist's realm of living things, the Indian has traditionally viewed the world of air, water, and minerals as alive: the river is (or has) a spirit, the big rock radiates energy, and even the humble clay has life.

It is easy for outsiders to become sentimental about this world view, something that Indians never would do. After all, Indians do kill animals, cut trees, burn grass, dig clay, and dam streams. The difference, perhaps, is that they do these things with a reciprocal attitude, with an understanding of the relationships between living things. They believe that they have permission to kill for food. Incorporating that belief into their daily living, they speak to an animal — partly to flatter, partly to apologize — before shooting it. They may offer tobacco smoke to a tree's spirit before cutting down the tree. A woman may talk to the clay she digs to make pots, explaining that she is taking no more than is necessary to sustain her family.

Indian culture sees a world full of living beings. Yet it does not view all living beings as having equal status or as worthy of equal consideration. For instance, Indians are only dimly aware of the life of the grass they walk on, but culture dictates that they are aware. A rabbit, unimportant most of the time, may suddenly communicate a vital message or bestow new power upon a human. Then there are the mighty beings, such as Sun and Eagle. This attitude shapes the religious practice of Indians. Obliged to communicate with a number of beings rather than just one, no part of their life is separated from feelings and practices that are easily classified as religious.

Sacred Power

In the academic study of religion, the term "Sacred Power" refers to whatever people try to control or relate to in order to achieve their religious goals. The exact description of Sacred Power differs from religion to religion. Sacred Power in the Christian religion is called "God" and is further described, in contrast to other similarly labeled beings, as having "sent his Son Jesus Christ" on an earthly mission for the benefit of human beings.

In contrast, Sacred Power in Indian religions is not spoken of as a single living being. It does not surprise us that in a world where life is everywhere, Power is also widely distributed rather than centrally focused. Here we get into trouble trying to describe the beliefs of all Indians at once. Not only are there different Indian beliefs but there is also little Indian testimony that has been recorded for the enlightenment of outsiders. Nevertheless, making allowance for endless variety and for our ignorance, we can observe that Indians conceive of Sacred Power on two interrelated levels.

Mana. On the most basic level, Sacred Power is a mysterious non-personal energy. Is it odd that Indians should conceive of anything as non-personal, when even a blade of grass has some whisper of personhood? Not necessarily, as virtually all Indians believe in a holy energy that has no personhood. But it may be added to a person's or object's own energy, normally with beneficial results. There are so many Indian names for this energy that we will use the anthropologist's term, *mana*, a name taken from the language of certain Pacific Island people who share a similar belief.

What is mana and how does it work, according to Indian belief? By itself, mana is not like a spirit or a god: it cannot know anything, decide anything, or promise anything. It cannot be loyal or treacherous, kind or cruel, friendly or hostile. It is pure energy, pure power, in some ways like electricity. People do not pray to it, though they may pray for it. According to Indians, mana is widely available, but it is probably not accurate to say that it is "everywhere," because mana is recognized only through particular day-to-day events. Whenever Indians encounter any display of special power, they attribute it to an increase in mana in that place, that object, or that person. For example, a plentiful harvest means that there is an increase of mana in the ground or in the crop. A stunning success — at war, hunting, or love — implies a surge of mana in persons or implements. Good luck is mana in operation. High performance of any kind is due to a concentration of mana. What we call personal qualities, such as talent, executive ability, sex appeal, and physical strength, are to the Indian all indicators of an inflow of mana to the fortunate person possessing such qualities.

Indians, then, have traditionally believed that obtaining and directing mana is the way to secure the welfare of the group and the personal goals of individuals. How do people get mana, and how do they direct it? You cannot appeal directly, because it cannot "hear"; it is non-personal. But there are other ways (remember the analogy with electricity). You can direct it by magic, special ceremonies or procedures for channeling mana, something like wiring your house for electric lights. You might "capture" the mysterious mana-power in small objects, called fetishes, which can be carried for various purposes. We will return to both of these methods shortly. Finally, Indians believe that they can receive mana from other persons, both human and non-human. Spirits and deities have great quantities of mana, which under certain conditions they will bestow upon human beings. Even though mana is non-personal and therefore deaf to your appeals, you can petition, in various ways, personal beings who have mana to give away. This is the bridge between Sacred Power as non-personal energy and Sacred Power as a crowd of personal beings.

Spirits and Deities. In Indian belief, spirits are invisible personal beings that frequently dwell inside visible objects. They are "personal " meaning that they have the characteristics of persons: they know they exist, they can make decisions, they can direct their own energy, they have likes and dislikes, and so forth. It is not surprising that the Indians' world is full of spirits, in view of the age-old belief that everything is alive. In Indian terms, if something is alive, it has a spirit. That formula applies to humans, animals, plants, mountains, rivers, and all other natural objects and phenomena.

In religion, spirits exist in a wide spectrum of powers and attitudes. Some are scarcely noticed, such as small plants and most insects. Some are dangerous, such as the spirits of recently deceased humans. Some are full of potential benefit: clouds, certain animals, healing herbs, and sometimes ancestors. Indian religion teaches how to approach these elusive but often friendly beings.

Sometimes a being is regarded as so powerful that we abandon the term "spirit" and call him or her a "deity," that is, a god or goddess. Not all Indian groups believe in deities, some confining their ideas of Sacred Power to mana and the spirits in their immediate environment. However, others — more often planters than hunter-gatherers — view Sun and Earth as deities. Still others have a notion of a chief deity, sometimes called "Great Spirit." Some Christian missionaries were delighted when they discovered this, because they thought that the Indians were very near to being Christians. Indians, too, have sometimes seen fit to minimize the difference between their traditional beliefs and the white people's religion. For our purposes, however, these differences should not be minimized. A minority of Indians believe in a chief deity worshiped exclusively, as the Christian, Jewish, and Muslim faiths require. Even in the presence of a Great Spirit, the religious energy of Indians is still directed toward a variety of beings.

Sacred Power: Special Cases

Taboo. Sacred Power is not always good or helpful. The term "taboo" refers to situations where Power is dangerous, and avoidance is the wise practice. ("Taboo," like "mana," is not an Indian word, but is widely used to refer to this aspect of Indian belief.)

Readers often have trouble with the idea of taboo, because in everyday speech the term is used more broadly than in careful studies of religion. For our purposes, "taboo" does not mean "forbidden." Among Indians, many things are forbidden by law and custom that are not taboo. When Indians say, "That is taboo," they are talking about something you should not touch, and perhaps not even look at or go near. If you do touch it, some danger will be present, or harm will occur. Depending on the situation, the harm may come to you, to the object touched, or to other members of your family, clan, or tribe.

At times, a taboo is connected with a mana-filled object, such as a medicine bundle or a ceremonial rattle. According to this belief, a person who touches the object without authority or without preparation will be inevitably harmed. The anticipated result is death, sickness, or loss of personal power.

Different sorts of taboo situations are usually connected with preparing for a special event in which great power is required, such as a hunt, a battle, or a religious ceremony. In these situations, certain foods may become temporarily taboo, along with certain animals, certain places, and perhaps members of the opposite sex. If they are touched during the crucial period, the event will lose power, and the group will suffer from bad hunting, defeated warriors, or an unproductive ceremony.

Special taboos surround the newly deceased. The corpse is taboo, and the area near it is also dangerous. Various beliefs explain fear of the dead. Many Indians have traditionally believed that the spirits of the newly dead are lonesome. The result: these spirits will attempt to get their loved ones to join them in the place of the dead. Whatever the reason, the dangerous power of the dead has to be separated from the living by means of a careful burial and mourning ceremonies involving temporary taboos. Gravediggers and corpse handlers may have to be isolated for a time in order to keep the community from "catching" death. Likewise, relatives of the deceased may have to avoid certain foods, associations, and localities, to protect themselves and others until the danger passes. After a while, the spirit of the deceased will grow happy in his or her new situation, or travel to a distant place, or simply lose the power to do harm.

Woman Power. Men have apparently always been impressed, and probably envious and frightened too, by women's ability to bear children. In Indian societies, where every new member greatly increased the chances for group survival, child-bearing was a spectacular event. So also was the related phenomenon, menstruation. It suggested that women had Power simply because they were women. The menstruating woman was a powerful being. But she and the men agreed that her Power did not mix well with the Power necessary for hunting and war. If she touched an arrow, it would not fly straight; if she crossed a deer trail, the deer would run away. Therefore, she must be secluded or restricted during her period; she was taboo. The restrictions varied: maintaining a separate hut, staying away from the sunlight, avoiding certain foods, not touching the men's food — the combinations are endless. "Don't you mind?" asked one anthropologist. "Mind!" was the response, "Why it's a holiday for us women. No work to do, no matter how the men may want it." But it wasn't always so jolly. Sometimes the restrictions were burdensome. Often the idea that a menstruating woman was sacred and powerful was converted to the notion that she was "unclean," making her restrictions a type of punishment. As time went on, these restrictions were greatly reduced. This frequently occurred in those tribes that became more prosperous, such as the fishermen of the northwest coast and the planters of the southeastern woodlands. However, practices connected with the power and danger of women have continued up to the present.

Fetishes. A fetish is a power-object containing mana. Indians have traditionally valued certain stones, feathers, sticks, bones, and other things for their power: to bring rain, game, or babies; to ward off disease, enemies, and storms. In short, these objects encourage good things and repel destroyers. Not long ago, an elderly Indian spotted a smooth, white stone among the rough, gray rocks of the desert. "I think this has power. Maybe it will bring rain." He whirled it clockwise around his head, stuck it in his pocket, and went home. When it rained generously that afternoon, the old man and his stone became the center of joyful attention. Of course, if the stone had not worked after two or three tries, he would have thrown it away.

Although such objects are regarded as powerful in their natural state, it often happens that fetishes must be manufactured by human knowledge and skill. Manufactured fetishes are often viewed as more potent or more precisely focused toward their particular objectives.

Thus, the bone is carved, and the feathers are notched and painted; plants are dried and mixed and sewn in a bag. These procedures might be accompanied by songs, or they might be carried out only at certain times of the day or month. A fetish is often connected with some powerful spirit. Most Indian groups include specialists who are trusted to make effective fetishes for the various purposes important to the group.

Visions. North American Indians developed a special belief in the relationship between visions and Sacred Power. The theory was as follows: a person could seek and receive a vision (or in some cases many visions in the course of a lifetime), which was actually a message or visitation from a powerful spirit, often appearing in the form of an animal. Sometimes the figure or figures in the vision gave spoken instructions; sometimes they performed a brief ritual or pantomime; sometimes they stood or sat in silence. Whatever the nature of the vision, it was understood to be a gift of Power to the human involved, but he or she must "follow" the vision by obeying the instructions and imitating the actions involved.

What Indians call visions, people with other points of view might call dreams or trances or hallucinations. Such familiar events as dreams are viewed by Indians as real and distinct from the mind that perceives them. In traditional Indian religion, people do not say, "It was only a dream." If this is true of an ordinary dream, how much more would it be true of the more vivid experience induced by lack of food, water, or sleep. This has been the most common way of seeking a power-vision. Parents instruct children and train them by stages to endure hunger, fatigue, and solitude necessary to the visionary experience.

In many Indian groups, the vision-seeking experiences were and are a moderately difficult part of progress toward adulthood. In the Plains tribes, on the other hand, the young male on the threshold of manhood engaged in an exceptionally grueling vision quest, which he believed would determine the quality of his remaining years. His future powers to hunt and fight, everything that gave honor to a Plains man, depended upon his vision. Seeking his vision amid severe, self-imposed rigors, as he had been taught, he anxiously pleaded with the spirits to grant him the required Power. When he returned to camp and reported his vision, wise men would comment on it and interpret it. But the only sure test was whether it worked. If he was afterward overcome with fear in combat, for instance, the failure would be attributed to the weakness of his vision. Among some groups, adults were encouraged to repeat the vision quest in order to renew or increase their powers. Medicine men and shamans sought visions repeatedly. For Indians in this country, the vision is a window in the partition between humans and the powerful beings through which Power flows to the seeker.

Indian Ritual

Ritual, a universal expression of religious belief and feeling, is the most common way that people approach Sacred Power. More precisely defined, ritual can be any repeated use of words, actions, and objects combined in a way that goes beyond ordinary significance and meaning. As an example, if you saw someone sweeping the front sidewalk, you would suppose that the broom was an ordinary household object being used in an ordinary way. If, however, you saw a person in white leather sweeping a large area of bare ground while timing the strokes to the beat of a drum, you would conclude that the sweeping was a ritual act and the broom was a ritual object.

From the Indian point of view, ritual is the principal way of manipulating mana and of maintaining contact with spirits and deities. Most Americans, even devoutly religious ones, have little patience with ritual, feeling that it is empty and wasted. They prefer their religious occasions to be "spontaneous." The Indian attitude could hardly be more different. They take comfort and gain confidence from familiar sounds and actions. As Ruth Underhill wrote,

> *Ceremonies great and small were the very fabric of life. They furnished the chief opportunities for learning, for feasting, for lovemaking. They gave courage to a lone hunter. They fused a group together in a heartening ritual. They combined the functions not only of a church but of a school, clinic, theater, and law court.*

Ritual is the road of life. Correctly performed, it draws holy Power into human hearts and human activities.

Made up of four elements, ritual is combined and varied in thousands of ways according to the group and the occasion. The first element is *movement*. We are aware of highly skilled Indian ritual dancers, but most ritual movement is very simple. For instance, it might consist of a measured walk with four pauses to the center of the ceremonial circle, then turning to offer a puff of smoke toward the Four Winds. Such actions are impressive only to those who know that every movement symbolizes a certain meaning and power. The second element is *song*. Prayers are usually given in the form of songs or chants that are believed to be full of power. They consist of short, repetitive phrases with a melody of four or five notes accompanied by drums. The third element is *story*. When a ritual includes stories, these may be traditional tales of gods, spirits, and heroes, as when some Indians annually recount the origins of the world. Or the stories may be recitals of important recent happenings, as in the case of some "first fruits" or thanksgiving rituals. The idea in both cases is that the power of the described event, whether ancient or modern, is bestowed upon the people who hear the story. The fourth element is *equipment*, such as paint, masks, aprons, fans, rattles, wands, and staffs. Viewed as power-objects, these items radiate energy and add to the power of the actions and sounds of the rituals.

Perhaps the most useful and customary dividing line we can draw concerning ritual is that between magic and worship. Although that simple classification presents some difficulties, it is still useful. Magical rituals are those in which the performer does not consciously appeal to a personal being; magic is non-personal, a matter-of-fact procedure. On the other hand, worship is any ritual in which the participants consciously direct their activity to spirits or deities. Worship may therefore provide, in addition to immediate practical benefits, more emotional and spiritual benefits than does magic. Although we will look at magic and worship separately, we should be aware that in practice they are not always so easily distinguishable. A single, long ceremony can easily alternate between magic and worship. The distinction often depends on the intention of the participant, which cannot be easily discerned by the observer. Nevertheless, there are times when the distinction is quite clear.

Magic. Sometimes viewed as a less exalted, less worthy activity than worship, magic is perhaps not religious at all. But if we are to say that religion consists of a people's dealing with non-ordinary or Sacred Power, and if that Power applies to practical matters as well as to fine thoughts, then it is hard to exclude magic or to regard it as inferior. (Of course, many non-Indians do not believe in magic, or in gods and spirits either, but that is a different matter, not now under discussion.)

The theory of magic is that certain ritual procedures will *automatically* direct Sacred Power. Pure magic is viewed much as we view the simple technique of turning on a light switch. No appeal is involved, no please and thank you. The simplest form of magic is the use of fetishes.

Sometimes these are used without any words or actions at all, as when a mother sews a squirrel's foot on her son's clothing to assist him in running. Sometimes the simplest action is involved, as when the old man whirled the rainstone around his head. Notice that in neither case is there an appeal to a supernatural being.

Yet a great deal of magic is more complicated than the simple use of a wonder-working object. Often there is a formula of words, called a "spell," which is used alone or in combination with objects and actions. Specialists, like shamans and medicine people, may have a number of spells for different needs. These they will teach for a fee. Other spells are passed along within families: "Your grandmother taught me to say this to ease the pain of childbirth." Sometimes the spell has passed from one language to another and is perhaps mispronounced, so that the syllables have no meaning except as a sequence of powerful sounds.

Magic can be used to induce harm as well as to help. For instance, a person may burn a bit of hair secretly acquired from a troublesome neighbor. The expected result is sickness or bad luck for the neighbor. Killing, on the other hand, is believed to require a magical technique unknown to most people, so a person would have to hire a specialist to do the job.

The job of magic is not an easy one. Magical rituals are sometimes more complex than the use of a simple fetish or the saying of a spell or the performance of a simple action. They can require all of the four ritual elements in a lengthy ceremony and can become intertwined with worship rituals. For instance, a specialist might complete a magical procedure and then recite a prayer or perform some other act of worship, asking the spirits to add their power to the power of the magic to make it more effective.

Worship. For our purposes, worship is an act in which people believe they are communicating with a living, personal Sacred Being. Whenever Indians approach spirits or deities, they are worshiping. It is possible, of course, to speak spontaneously to such a being, and Indians sometimes do that. But usually they have greater confidence if the approach is made through ritualized movement, songs, stories, and objects, combined in patterns hallowed with age.

As a general rule, planting societies developed more frequent and elaborate worship (or mixed worship-magic) rituals than hunter-gatherers did. This was not only because the growth cycle of the crops provided important occasions for ritual, but also because farming communities have more leisure and resources for ceremony. Typical planting communities schedule their acts of worship according to a calendar based on careful observations of the sun. Thus, the Hopi ritual year begins with several days of ceremony leading up to the winter solstice, the day when the sun is "weakest." On that occasion, a dancer with a shield representing the sun dances vigorously and twirls the shield, in order to make the sun strong again, enabling it to foster the growth of crops in the spring and summer. Another period of Hopi ceremony, this time in the spring, focuses upon reverence to snake-spirits, who are bringers of rain and fertility. Among the acts of worship are dancing with live snakes and a drama complete with impressive snake puppets.

The Hopi are famous for fine dancing and pageantry, but the power of the ritual should not be judged by its impression on outsiders. The ritual is effective when people know and feel the meaning of every simple gesture and every humble object that is used. Ritual is powerful for those who can feel the drama of a song repeated fifty-six times. That requires sensitivity of a sort not often found in an industrial society.

Religious Specialists

Indian communities have traditionally included people who are believed to possess the special sensitivities and abilities for channeling Sacred Power to meet people's needs. The most important specialists are called shamans, medicine men (women), and priests. Sometimes these functions are combined in a single person, but we shall describe each separately.

Both shamans and medicine persons receive their power from contact with spirits. And they each have similar functions, consisting of healing diseases and performing other services for the well-being of the community. Of the two, shamans are more spectacular in their claims and performances, while medicine people are more restrained and dignified.

Shamans are people who believe that they have died and are reborn. It is this experience which enables them to go into trances whenever they choose. In a trance, their spirits are in touch with other powerful spirits who will assist them. Whenever a shaman works, the event is marked by strange sounds, including the voices of the different spirits involved in the event. The theory behind each of the shaman's operations is that spirits are traveling around getting the job done. For example, when a person is ill, the shaman will diagnose the cause as the loss of soul, perhaps as the result of the person's violation of a taboo, or an enemy's theft of the soul. In an impressive and often lengthy ceremony, one or more shamans will send their spirits, or their helper-spirits, out to search for the lost soul and bring it back. Then, a shaman will insert it through the back of the sick person's head. If the problem is locating animals to hunt, the shaman sends his spirit flying in all directions until he can "see" the game. The spirit returns, and the shaman directs the hunters. Forecasting is not ignored: the shamans also believe that they can predict the future by calling on a well-informed spirit. This spirit enters the shaman's body and speaks through his or her mouth.

Medicine persons (usually men but occasionally older women) receive their power through visions repeated or renewed fairly often. Unlike shamans, the medicine persons do not work in a trance state. Believing their visions give them power to cure diseases and do other valuable things, they apply it without going into a trance. For instance, when they heal, they use combinations of ceremonial magic, appeal to spirits, power-objects, and herbal remedies. According to one theory of disease that many medicine men use, illness is caused by some foreign object, maybe a stick or a worm, that has entered the body by accident or by evil magic. In such cases, the medicine person begins by using a rock crystal to locate the disease-object, continues for hours or days in ceremony, and finally uses a cup or tube to suck out the object. This sucking cure is well-known among most of the Indians of North America, and it apparently goes back to the people who migrated from Asia several thousands of years ago.

Different from the other two specialists are priests, for their authority does not depend on visions or trances. Priests are men who have been trained to perform and lead the ceremonies of worship that are highly valued in some Indian groups. Historically, big public worship ceremonies appeared mainly in agricultural tribes; therefore, those are the groups that produced fully developed priesthoods. That means that priests are the latest Indian religious specialists to arise in North America. They appeared fifteen to twenty centuries ago, while shamans have been around for 10,000 years or so, and medicine men and women have existed for perhaps twice that long. The priests, then, were and are those who know exactly how to prepare and conduct every segment of a week-long thansgiving ceremony or a spring fertility ritual. Between the great rituals, priests are the ones who offer daily worship at the shrines of the gods and goddesses. That function requires training, concentration, and dedication rather than visionary power. The responsibility of a priest is immense, because the welfare of the entire community depends on performing the ceremonies without mistake — or at least knowing how to undo mistakes that are made.

Having separately described shaman, medicine person, and priest, one must unfortunately go on to say that these three specialist roles often are combined in ways that are hard to classify. First, any hunter-gatherer group would have to have at least one shaman or medicine man. A group would not require both types of specialists, because each type can perform the same services, such as healing. In general, Arctic and Subarctic groups have tended to produce shaman-type specialists, while tribes in the area of the continental United States produced medicine-type practitioners. But there was a broad and shifting borderland between the two areas, where specialists had some features of *both* types. For instance, the Ojibway specialist traditionally combined the spirit-flight technique for guiding hunters with the sucking cure for healing diseases. Besides that, both shamans and medicine people are noted for making fetishes and prescribing spells for many purposes according to the client's need.

Finally, it is reasonable to suppose that the earliest priests were also medicine people or shamans; that is, people who were already religious leaders were the ones who developed the priestly role when the need arose. As they did the priestly business, it is not likely that they stopped doing the other things. The priestly role might be dominant, but they could still work a cure or make a fetish. Therefore, there were and are priest-medicine men and priest-shaman-medicine men, in the same way that specialists in other religions combine several roles in one individual. On the other hand, a group might be large enough to have several religious experts, each rather narrowly specialized. The Navahos even have people whose special function is to diagnose a person's trouble and then recommend the appropriate specialist, healer or ceremonialist, to deal with the problem.

Encounter With the White World

The coming of Europeans to this continent and the establishment of the United States of America led to disaster for Indians. In order to understand the religious results of that disaster, we should look first at other dimensions of the red-white collision.

The terms of the conflict were set by the British colonists. Although a few of the early settlers dreamed of fortunes in gold, they quickly became dependent upon agriculture, both to feed themselves and to produce staple products for trade. Farmers have ideas about land use and property rights that are different from the ideas of hunter-gatherers. Farmers cannot tolerate much hunting, because it disturbs the crops, and farming drives away game animals and destroys wild plants. Wherever there was a colonial farm or plantation, Indians were dispossessed.

You might ask if this fact alone induced the decline. The answer would, of course, be in the negative, for the mere presence of white farmers did not disrupt the culture of a continent. After all, many Indians were farmers too. Far from the idyllic portrayals, Indians had been dispossessing Indians for centuries. As humans seem inclined to do, they stole from each other, enslaved each other, and killed each other. They were no strangers to forced migration and forced changes in their lifeways. How was the white assault different? The answer to that question, and to the sad question of the disaster of the Indians, is simply that the whites were so numerous. By 1750, there were more Europeans in the British colonies than there were Indians in all of America north of Mexico. By the time of the first U.S. census in 1790, there were three million whites in the new nation and probably no more than a million Indians in all of the United States and Canada. In the nineteenth century, the rate of European immigration rose sharply. With the Indian population diminishing, the total U.S. population rose to 32 million by 1861 and 76 million by 1900.

More people required more land, and they applied relentless pressure to get it. "Brush aside and override" is the way one writer describes the process. "One thing about white people," says Old Lodge Skins in *Little Big Man*, "they won't go away." The only thing that could have stopped white movement was a much larger military force than the Indians could muster. As it was, changes were forced upon Indians many times faster than ever before. In the last two centuries, Indians have been required to respond to greater change than in all the previous thousand years. Traders and missionaries were agents of change before the soldiers came. Many leading Indians, particularly in the South, had adopted the living style of upper-class whites, including converting to Christianity and sending their children to the best white schools, all while remaining the active leaders of their people. Others were changed by trade goods, such as fabrics, beads, steel blades and points, guns, and liquor. But, of course, greater changes came about by force: new patterns of work (or forced inactivity), disruption of family life, and loss of religious leaders.

The thin line of colonial settlements began in the seventeenth century. Nowhere were the relations of Indians and colonists very good. In each place, open hostilities began within a decade after first settlement. The Europeans were so few that it seems incredible that they were not destroyed at the very beginning. But apparently the eastern seaboard had slumped to a low point of Indian population, so the force was not there. And, of course, the colonists fought very hard, because there was no retreating. By the time of the Revolution, the eastern Indians had drawn back, resettling in the mountains that for a time blocked white migration westward. Formerly separate tribes merged or formed alliances in a process repeated many times afterward under white pressure.

After the Revolution, white settlers streamed across the mountains and began filling the valleys between the Appalachians and the Mississippi River. Indians were defeated and withdrew from these lands, although some stayed behind on reservations or in isolated places. The best documented removal was that of the Cherokees, whose Trail of Tears stretched from Georgia to Oklahoma in the latter 1830s. By this time, most whites agreed that Indians were greatly inferior to the European stock. At best, they were childish; at worst, cruelly barbaric. There was nothing to be learned from them — nothing about them was worthy of white respect or consideration. The only thing they possessed of value was the land they occupied.

For the white culture, the westward thrust continued. The United States purchased Louisiana, which stretched from the Mississippi to the Pacific Northwest. Lewis and Clark explored a route from St. Louis to the Pacific in 1804-1805. In the 1840s, the pattern of annexation, conquest, and treaty completed the western territory of the United States, except for the southern part of Arizona and New Mexico. This was purchased in 1853. Hastening the white movement westward was the Gold Rush of 1849. Indians who had scarcely settled into the Great Plains found themselves challenged by wagon trains and newly constructed forts. Treaties were signed and reservations established, but the Civil War forced the federal government to withdraw its troops, allowing a brief regrowth of Plains culture.

Immediately after the Civil War, the great western project started — the railroad. Huge buffalo herds, on which Plains life depended, slowed construction and stopped trains. Therefore, they were summarily eliminated by soldiers, settlers, and hired hunters, from 1870 to 1872. The Plains people went hungry and cold. And, despite Indian victories, including annihilating Custer's Seventh Calvary, the 1870s and 1880s brought an end to the familiar living patterns of the Plains tribes. By the end of the century, the remaining tribes farther west had also lost their own independence.

Sooner or later, every tribe in a single generation had experienced every kind of human catastrophe: betrayal and humiliation, forced marches and death of loved ones, disease, and massacre. Births diminished; deaths multiplied. At the low point, around 1880, there were only 250,000 Indians. In 1800, few white Americans could have imagined or intended the disaster they would soon bring upon the Indians. By 1900, not many were troubled by the sorry result.

The history of legislative and bureaucratic planned treatment of Indians in the last hundred years is sometimes as sad as their reckless treatment by the Army. It is a story of ignorance and mismanagement, alternating with sensitivity and selfless devotion. Even private religious agencies, both Catholic and Protestant, have a mixed record in their work among Indians. Such a story cannot instill optimism within the foreseeable future, but it does have happy features. In the last century, the Indian population has tripled or quadrupled. By the usual estimates, there are about as many Indians in the United States today as there were when the colonists first came. As the threat of physical extinction fades into the background, the extremely poor material conditions of the contemporary Indian life continues. But, despite many casualties, Indians have refused to die culturally, politically, and mentally. Creating different kinds of movements to foster self-esteem, cultural renaissance and civil rights, they are still resisting, still fighting a conflict in which survival is the victory. Religious patterns, new and old, are part of the struggle.

Encounter With Christianity

Christianity was the religion of the white world. Indians confronted it as soon as the Europeans arrived. People will disagree as to whether the missionaries were agents of conquest as much as the soldiers were, or whether they managed in some cases to alleviate the worst effects of the conquest. There is evidence on both sides. The results of their work could be good or bad, but nearly all missionaries sincerely intended to help the Indians, both in this life and, more importantly for the missionary, in the afterworld.

When the Spanish and the French came to the New World, priests and Indian missions had an integral role in the colonizing venture. However, for the British, Indian missions were not so important. They usually depended on the zeal of clergyman whose main duty was to the colonists. There were a few dedicated missionaries in the colonial period. English-speaking Protestant missions did not really get moving until the nineteenth century, sometimes with the support of the federal government. By that time, French-speaking Catholic missions south of Canada had nearly disappeared, while most Spanish and Mexican priests withdrew in the face of American sovereignty, leaving their followers in a weak religious position.

Although there were differences between Catholics and Protestants in their approach to the Indians, all missionaries went about their work with two goals in mind: converting the Indians and civilizing them. The assumption of nearly all missionaries was clear: Indian religion produced barbaric behavior in this life and eternal punishment in the next. The old ways had to be uprooted and replaced. In short, Indians had to be converted to the Christian faith. In addition, their "habits of life" had to be exchanged for the superior ways of white civilization: reading and writing, plow and churn, soap and water, trousers and dresses. In some circles, there was considerable debate about "christianizing" and "civilizing." Did you convert a savage first and then teach him table manners, or were the basic rules of white living necessary to prepare him for Christian faith? The debate was settled in practice by pursuing both objectives at the same time.

Take nineteenth-century Protestant missions as an example. The center of activity was the mission station, a cluster of buildings serving as residence, school, chapel, and barn, all in the midst of mission-owned farm land sometimes located near Indian villages. Some work was directed toward adults, but mission strategy at that time among Protestants was centered upon children. After all, they were easier to "mold." The best educational theory of the time encouraged teachers to "mold the habits" of their pupils, whether red, black, or white. So the missionaries persuaded parents to send their children to the mission school. There they were taught hygiene, reading and writing, arithmetic, and Christian doctrine. The girls were instructed in homemaking and the boys in farming. There were also religious services.

When this education was successful, the children were

put at odds with their parents, who could counter by withdrawing their children from school. The solution was simple: the missionaries agreed that boarding schools were better than day schools, for pupils needed to be away from the undesirable influence of their parents. The system worked best when parents understood and approved of the objectives of the school, which was more likely to occur before 1830, among eastern farming Indians. They had friendly contacts with white people and admired some features of white society. Sometimes a school ended up mainly teaching the children of converted adults. On the other hand, the system at its worst received pupils whose parents were coerced by government agents into sending them. Although missionaries may have felt they were saving children, the youngsters were virtual hostages in exchange for the peaceable behavior of their parents.

What was the Indian response to the missionaries? Probably most Indians were dimly aware of Christianity and made no choice at all. Others saw the challenge and rejected the white man's religion. They recognized that Christianity required the end of Indian life as they knew it. As one group phrased it (Berkhofer, 107):

> *White men were made wearing clothes to work. It is proper for them to plough, build houses, etc. But we are made naked to dance, hunt, and go to war. If we should abandon the customs of our ancestors, the Wakan would be angry at us and we would die.*

Other Indians became Christians and sought to shape their lives according to the missionaries' teaching. There were features of Christianity that were appealing to some Indians. In Catholicism, they saw sacred drama and holy objects something like those of their own people. In Protestantism, they were impressed by churchly sounds: the portable organ, the hymn singing, and the measured cadence of a good sermon. Also, it was obvious to Indians that white people, though puzzling and often treacherous, were clever and powerful. Perhaps this power came from their religion, which thus might be good for Indians too. There was no denying that Christians seemed very sure about seeing loved ones in heaven. That was an attractive point at a time when many Indians were dying.

Another response to Christianity was to blend Christian features with traditional Indian features, resulting in a new and satisfying religious pattern. Some of the most successful examples are in the Southwest, but it must not be supposed that either Catholic or Indian priests favored this type of thing at first. In the twentieth century, one may see a saint's image smiling down upon a midsummer green corn festival. At Christmas time, Pueblo Deer Dancers in full regalia enter the church in procession and kneel before the infant Christ in the manger. Other examples of this sort of integration are described in the next section.

Survival and Renewal: Religion After The Conquest

The crisis in Indian life caused by white conquest was also religious in nature. Much that gave comfort and courage to Indian people was destroyed. Sacred places were lost when Indians were forced to relocate. Priests and medicine men, often the oldest members of the group, were killed or died without training successors. Ritual objects vanished in smoke as soldiers burned the villages. Worst of all, people lost confidence in the ceremonies that had brought harmony and well-being to their lives. The holy ways had evidently lost their power, or else the Indians would have won.

However, Indians could not remain always in such an anxious state of mind. One of the assumptions of religious scholarship is that people crave harmony and equilibrium in their lives, and they strive to achieve it with whatever resources they have. Often the result is some sort of religious structure. Many Indians succeeded in finding something of the harmony that was disrupted by white violence and contempt.

One path followed by many Indians today is to pursue the traditional ways faithfully. This does not mean slavishly "preserving" the old ways. These are living practices full of contemporary meaning. Ruth Underhill (1-2) describes a ceremony on the northwest coast. Fires are burning on the earthen floor of the large dance house; people are sitting around the walls on bleachers; men are drumming on the rafters with long poles. Suddenly one man gets up and runs down the room circling the fires and chanting, "Enemy come! Enemy come!" Dr. Underhill continues:

> *"He has got the war spirit", said my Indian neighbor reverently, "It's rare. Powerful."*
> *"But there is no war now."*
> *"Spirit is powerful for lots of things. His grandfather had it. Oh, this is good! We feared no one would get a spirit this year."*

The neighbor who told me this was glowing with enthusiasm. A spark of hope and confidence had been lighted in him and in that whole roomful of modern Indians.

Similarly, the many Chants or Sings of the Navaho people are used to combat not only physical ailments but also the more elusive soul sicknesses of the modern world. "It is finished in beauty," chants the joyful patient, echoed by scores or hundreds of guests, who share the blessing.

In addition to the traditional ceremonies, Indians also developed new religions during the last two centuries. These are sometimes called "nativistic" or "revitalizing" religions, because they promise recovery from the suffering caused by whites. These religious movements were often connected with the message of a prophet or a messiah. Some of them lasted only a few years, while others have endured a long time and, in some cases, are still growing. Some of them have been limited to a single tribe, but others have been "pan-Indian" religions, meaning that they are open to all Indians.

Some of these revitalization movements taught that the white invaders would be defeated or supernaturally extinguished, if the Indians would follow certain teachings. The earliest recorded example of this was the religion of the "Delaware Prophet" near Lake Erie in 1762. This and some other early movements taught that Indians would arise and defeat the whites. Understandably, they lost influence after major white victories. According to later prophets, there would be a supernatural upheaval, in which the world would be destroyed and remade, and the whites would disappear. (Note the parallel with the Christian idea of the "end of the world," in which the devil and his servants are to be destroyed or removed.)

The best-documented example of this was the Ghost Dance movement. This movement arose in Nevada under the prophet Wodzuwob (Tavibo) in 1869 and spread to California. After losing influence, it developed again in Nevada in 1886 under the preaching of the prophet Wowoka, who said he had twice experienced death and resurrection. God had told him that the earth would soon be covered by a tide of mud and water. But if the Indians danced and sang according to instructions, the tide would pass under them. They would survive, but the whites would be destroyed. Furthermore, the Indian dead would return and join the dance. Wowoka's religion spread to the recently subdued groups on the Great Plains, where hundreds of people each night joined the dancing. "The rocks are ringing," they sang. "The earth will tremble." Whites became nervous as the Indians grew so excited. Newspapers printed inflammatory accounts. The result was the murder of Sitting Bull and the massacre of 300 Indians at Wounded Knee in 1890. Since that time no more "hostile" prophets have appeared. In some ways, the Indian militants of the last twenty years are their successors.

Parallel with the prophets of white demise were several revitalization movements that emphasized peaceful coexistence with whites and the perpetuation of traditional Indian life. Indians would be strengthened with beauty and power. White oppressors would be ignored or perhaps prayed for. The earliest known example of this form of religious movement was connected with the Iroquois prophet Ganioda'yo (Handsome Lake) beginning in 1789. He taught peace with the whites, together with a rededication to certain old ceremonies that he specified. The rituals that he revived have been followed by many Iroquois groups ever since.

Later, on the west coast, several religious practices grew using religious objects borrowed from Christianity, particularly the cross and the brass hand bell used in Catholic mission schools. The most durable of these movements, surviving to the present, was the Indian Shaker Church, founded in 1882 by a Squaxin Indian named John Slocum. Like Wowoka a few years later, Slocum twice experienced death and resurrection. In a reversal of Handsome Lake's message a century earlier, Slocum taught that Indians must give up the old ceremonies, especially those connected with shamanism. Instead, Indians should await the voices of God and Jesus, who had messages especially for Indians and not for whites. Indian Shaker churches were built, complete with steeples, crosses, and bells. Shaker ceremony includes dignified processions, chanting, and bell-ringing. The leader speaks in a low voice, like a spirit-possessed shaman, while an interpreter repeats his words. Sometimes worshipers tremble or shake, and this is taken as a sign of spiritual power. The Indian Shakers have a reputation as healers and miracle workers, and even some non-Shaker Indians will seek their help in time of illness.

Of all the new-old religions of revitalization, the peyote movement is the largest and fastest growing. Peyote is a cactus that produces little bulbs or buttons. These buttons are eaten at peyote ceremonies and are carried as power-objects. The peyote root also has religious uses and contains mescaline, which produces experiences that unbelievers call hallucinations and believers call visions. Worshipers usually eat relatively small quantities of peyote in their ceremonies.

The religious use of peyote goes back at least 400 years to the Aztecs and other Indian groups in Mexico. Coming to the United States about a hundred years ago, it started in Oklahoma, where special ceremonies appeared in which peyote was the central feature. These ceremonies spread throughout the Southwest and northward through the Plains. The "peyote way" was organized into the Native American Church in 1918, but no one organization can contain it. There are now associations of peyote churches, of which the largest is the intertribal, international federation known as the Native American Church of North America. In some jurisdictions, the courts permit the use of peyote by members of the Native American Church, while banning it for the rest of the population. Peyotists approve of this distinction, believing that only Indians can learn to use the substance reverently.

"Long ago God took pity on the Indian," says one peyotist (Slotkin, 520) who is also an anthropologist. "So God created Peyote and put some of his power into it for the use of Indians." For a believer, Peyote begins with a capital letter, for it is not merely the name of cactus but also the power within the cactus. The Peyote Road is a good road, believers say, but a hard one too. Followers should not use alcohol. They should work hard and they should not quarrel.

Peyote is normally taken in solemn all-night ceremonies. These are held usually in Plains-type tipis, built facing east and furnished with special ritual objects. Worshipers must come freshly bathed and in clean clothes. They are purified with cedar smoke. They eat Peyote and confess their sins. They sing, among many songs, "I walk the Peyote Road. It is a good road." They contemplate the strange ways of the world while rejoicing in the Power that strengthens them and leads them through the struggle. At dawn they share a meal of traditional Indian foods, offer a final prayer, and move out toward the rising sun.

Selected People and Events

26000 B.C.	Start of a 5,000 year period when conditions were favorable for land migration from Siberia to Alaska, and probable period of arrival of the first "Old Indians" in North America.
11000 B.C.	Beginning of a final 3,000 year period of land migration, ending when the Bering Platform is submerged around 8000 B.C.
7000 B.C.	"Old Indians" reach the tip of South America.
5000 B.C.	Beginning of corn-growing in Mexico, transforming the culture of many groups in Mexico by 1500 B.C.
1 A.D.	Corn is introduced into the area of the future United States.
500 A.D.	Beginning of the Middle Mississippi culture, corn growers and builders of temple pyramids resembling those of the Aztecs.
1493	Christopher Columbus establishes a Spanish settlement on the island of Hispaniola, the beginning of continuous European settlement in the Western Hemisphere.
1607	Beginning of continuous British settlement within the area of the future United States.
1680	Pueblo rebellion against Spanish rule contributing to the acquisition of horses by Indians.
1762	The "Delaware Prophet" near Lake Erie preaches the defeat of the whites.
1778	The first treaty of the United States of America with an Indian tribe.
1789	The Iroquois prophet Ganioda'yo (Handsome Lake) preaches peace with the whites and revival of traditional ceremonies.
1795	Tenskwatawa, a Shawnee prophet of the Ohio Valley, preaches defeat of the whites, promising Indian warriors immunity against bullets.
1804	Sacajawea, a Shoshoni woman, guides the Lewis Clark expedition up the Missouri River.

1817 Andrew Jackson, future President, writes that he views treaties with the Indians as an "absurdity not to be reconciled to the principles of our government."

1821 The Cherokee alphabet, invented by Sequoyah, is approved by the tribal council, and thousands of people quickly learn to read and write.

1869 Beginning of the Ghost Dance religion under the Paiute prophet Wodzuwob.

1882 Establishment of the Indian Shaker Church, led by John Slocum.

1885 Approximate time when Peyote was introduced into the United States.

1886 Revival of the Ghost Dance religion by the Paiute prophet Wowoka, who is joined by many Plains people until the Wounded Knee massacre, December 29, 1890.

1918 Organization of the Native American Church, based on Peyote ceremony.

1924 Congress extends United States citizenship to all Indians born in the United States.

1931 Black Elk, an aging priest of the Oglala Sioux, narrates to John G. Neihardt the story of his life and vision, published as *Black Elk Speaks*, the most widely read testimony by an Indian religious leader.

1944 Formation of the National Congress of American Indians, a nationwide tribal alliance.

1948 Indians win court cases challenging discriminatory voting regulations in Arizona and New Mexico.

1950 Beginning of a period of religious renewal among Indians, including renewed commitment to traditional ceremonies and rapid spread of the peyote groups, coinciding with a congressional campaign to "detribalize" Indians and end federal assistance.

1961 The American Indian Chicago Conference, the first national gathering of young Indian leaders.

1969 Beginning of a nineteen-month occupation of Alcatraz Island by Indian activists, which sharpens national awareness of all Indian existence.

1972 The Trail of Broken Treaties demonstration, culminating in the week-long occupation of the Bureau of Indian Affairs offices in Washington by 500 Indians.

1973 Three-month occupation of the village of Wounded Knee, South Dakota, by armed Indians protesting treaty violations.

CHAPTER THREE

White Protestantism: Consensus and Conflict

The great majority of Christians around the world belong to one of three major branches of Christianity. About fifty-five percent of the world's approximately one billion Christians belong to the Roman Catholic Church. Protestantism, made up of many independent denominations, accounts for about one quarter of the Christian population, while the several Eastern Orthodox jurisdictions account for most of the remainder. As we saw in Chapter 1, these proportions are different in the United States, where two thirds of the population identify themselves as Protestants of one kind or another, one quarter as Roman Catholics, and less than two percent as Eastern Orthodox in their religious belief.

What accounts for this pattern of religious distribution? The answer can be traced back to the pattern of European migration to North America. At the time of the Revolution, nearly all of the European-derived portion of the population were of Protestant ethnic groups: English, Scotch-Irish, Scottish, or German (from Protestant parts of Germany — Catholic Germans came later). These nationalities continued to account for nearly all newly arrived Americans through the 1820s. Only after 1830 did Catholics compose the majority of new arrivals. By that time, Protestant pre-eminence was solidly established.

The Varieties of Protestantism

One of the most bewildering features of American

Protestantism is the large number of separate groups included in it. Nearly three hundred Protestant denominations exist in the United States today, ranging in size from a hundred members to thirteen million. The picture is simplified, however, if we group the denominations according to family names. Various groups of Baptists, Methodists, Lutherans, and Presbyterians now make up about two thirds of the Protestant population. If we added another half-dozen names to the list, we would account for ninety-five percent of American Protestants.

Still, it is not surprising that people sometimes wonder why there are so many groups. Some of the reasons stem from the origins of Protestantism in sixteenth century Europe. In that century, Protestant movements developed independently in several places. Examples include the Lutheran churches, originating in Germany, and the Calvinist or Reformed churches, originating in Switzerland. Although they influenced each other, they did not join in a single organization. In each new country where these movements spread, separate organizations developed. For instance, independent Lutheran churches arose in Sweden, Norway, Denmark, and Finland. Calvinist expansion also produced independent churches, such as the Dutch Reformed Church and the Scottish Presbyterians. As long as Europeans stayed in Europe, there was usually one Protestant organization in each region. But during the trans-Atlantic migrations, representatives of all the groups found their way to America. Because it is not easy to unite groups of different national origins even when they are very similar, the various denominations often remained separate in the New World.

Besides the groups that evolved through the accidents of geography, disputes about belief and practice also paved the way for some groups to split from parent bodies. For instance, questions of church government — that is, how God wants Christians to organize the churches — were frequent sources of conflict. There are three basic types of church government: episcopal, presbyterian, and congregational. Most Protestants over the years have been convinced that one or another of these is the one desired by God. The episcopal type of church is governed by officers called bishops who are sometimes believed to have special authority handed down through the centuries from Christ and the Apostles. In this country, the Methodists and Episcopalians provide examples of episcopal government. The presbyterian type rejects bishops in favor of government by committees, called presbyteries. A presbytery exercises certain kinds of authority over a group of congregations. Any denomination with Presbyterian or Reformed in its name is an example of presbyterian government. Churches of the congregational type believe that church decisions should be made by the vote of all the members: no bishops, no presbyteries. Each congregation is independent and self-governing. Congregationalists (now mostly merged with the United Church of Christ), Baptists, and Disciples of Christ are examples of this type.

A third and final reason for the large number of Protestant denominations in America is that after the Revolution the Constitution and Bill of Rights provided for full religious liberty to all, which we will look at later in the chapter. One result of this infusion of religious liberty was to remove all legal restrictions against forming new religious bodies. What better opportunity could people who strongly disagreed with an existing denomination have than to exercise their newly found liberty and secede from their former church and start their own? Thus, church organization and other basic beliefs potentially reflect the deep conviction of the believers, causing lasting disagreement and division. This divisive activity, however, has been counteracted in American Protestant history by the process of merger and reunion, one of the most important facets of the American Protestant experience.

The Puritan Heritage

The fact that the early immigrants were English meant that the affairs of the Church of England (whose members are called Anglicans) played a large role in determining the type of Protestantism important in the New World. The most vigorous movement within the Church of England in the seventeenth century was Puritanism. Notably, this odd term never referred to any particular church organization but to a religious movement that promoted Calvinist or Reformed principles within the existing Church of England.

Puritans believed that the Church of England, which has separated from Rome in 1534, had not gone far enough in purging itself from the supposed evils of Roman Catholicism. They demanded specific reforms in the areas of worship, doctrine, and daily life. Because this was a national church, governed by King and Parliament as well as by clergy, the Puritans attempted to alter the church through political means, such as by using petition legislation, and revolution. For a time, they ruled England.

In America, a large portion of the colonists from Britain and Northern Ireland were Puritans or were sympathetic with Puritan principles. Not only did Puritans found the Congregationalist churches of New England, but their influence was also strong in other groups throughout the colonies. Such British-derived groups as Presbyterians, Baptists, Friends (Quakers), and Methodists though disagreeing with the Congregationalists on some points, shared the basic Puritan ideas. Thus, within a decently firm definition of the term, we can identify most colonial American religion as not merely Protestant but as specifically Puritan. Because so much of American Protestantism has roots in the Puritan movement, it is helpful to look at what Puritans believed were the essential features of true Christianity.

In the first place, they believed that the Bible was the only source of authority in human affairs. All true teaching and right living springs from the Holy Scriptures. To justify their doctrines and their laws by reference to particular passsages in the Bible was part of the Puritan belief. Much of their program of religious reform consisted of sweeping away those features of earlier (Catholic or "papist") church life that could not, in their judgment, meet this test. Banned from the Puritan circle were the vestments worn by priests, the practice of kneeling for Holy Communion, and many other features of Roman Catholicism, and of Anglicanism as well. The first law code in the Puritan Commonwealth of Massachusetts, called the Body of Liberties (1641), included marginal notes indicating the Biblical foundation for the various statutes.

Secondly, Puritans believed that Christianity is a reasonable religion. To be sure, they said that the basic truths are revealed by God in the Bible because the unaided human mind could not discover them alone. Yet they viewed the whole Christian system as acceptable to sound thinking, as "agreeable to reason." Christian teaching was supposed to make sense; Puritans had no fondness for "blind faith." Ministers prided themselves on their ability to make deep ideas understandable to farmers, artisans, and housewives, who for their part listened attentively, discussed religious teachings among themselves, and explained them to their children. In order to become a church member, a person had to demonstrate what was called "general faith" or "historical faith." That is, he or she had to stand up in church and give an orderly account of basic Christian doctrines as learned from parents and ministers. Because true religion was reasonable religion, Puritans placed a high value on education. A man was not considered an acceptable minister unless he had a university education. The immigrant ministers in New England were university graduates, and they quickly founded colleges in order to guarantee the continuation of an educated ministry. Even lay people were expected to have an elementary education, so that they could read the Bible and other spiritual literature, and be intelligent teachers of their own children. This expectation led to the founding of schools accessible to the majority of the population under Puritan influence.

A third, well-known feature of Puritan life was its emphasis on simplicity and even austerity. In daily life, it meant the absence of personal adornment — frills, jewelry, and the like (not that most of the people could afford such things). In religion, it meant no dramatic elements in the worship services, such as the complex movements of the Catholic Mass, and no "visual aids" to worship, such as colorful vestments or religious pictures and statues. The bare room of the Puritan church building, or "meeting house," contained only seats, a pulpit, and perhaps, a table from which Holy Communion was served. Even when later generations became more prosperous and churches more expensive, the beauty of simple architectural forms devoid of stained glass, paintings, or sculpture was retained.

Fourthly, Puritans believed in "saving faith". This idea applied to church life in a special way. Saving faith was understood to be different from general faith, which we noted was acquired through instruction by parents and ministers. Saving faith was not directly related to instruction or to statements of doctrine. It was seen as an inward experience, the result of God's mercy operating in one's soul. The way you might know you had it was if, after being deeply convinced of your sinfulness ("conviction"), you began to believe that Christ's merits could overcome your sin and save you from damnation ("saving faith"). This was not the same as believing *generally* in the goodness of God or the sacrifice of Christ. You had to feel that these things were applied *particularly* to your own sins. After a while, it became a requirement for membership in most Puritan churches that the candidate tell the story of his or her own inner struggles and convince the congregation that the gift of saving grace had been received. This requirement of testifying to the experience of saving faith became very important in many Protestant churches.

A fifth aspect of Puritanism was close attention to the behavior of church members. The general tendency was, in Puritan churches, to limit membership to those who were free from open, identifiable sin. In other words, one had to show a certain type of behavior to get into the church and also to stay in. In general, these Puritan standards were directed toward maintaining a harmonious, family-oriented, religiously serious community. Specifically, one should attend Sunday church services, avoid drunkenness and malicious gossip, be honest in business dealings, and limit sexual activity to one's marriage partner. People who showed off in dress or manner, or who idled away time in games and bawdy singing, aroused suspicion. However, this attitude did not, contrary to popular belief, restrain Puritans from enjoying fun and good humor. They even had a few drinks on many occasions connected with work projects and church entertainments. The important point to be made is that if one's behavior violated church standards, he or she would not be admitted to church membership. Once within the church, a person could be charged with a misbehavior and be asked to correct the misdeed. If one refused to do so or became a habitual offender, the result was expulsion from the list of church members, so that the offender might be shocked or shamed into repentance and the church would not be brought into disrepute.

Finally, an important trait of the Puritan version of Christianity was the conviction on the part of the members that they were especially chosen by God for some high purpose. John Winthrop, first governor of Massachusetts, urged his shipboard companions on the way to America to remember "that we shall be as a City upon a Hill, the eyes of all people are upon us." Their task was no less than to construct and maintain a model Christian society, cleansed of impurities of life and doctrine that remained in the unreformed churches. God was granting special protection to the colonists, just as he had chosen and protected the ancient Children of Israel. Such special favor requires special effort from God's people. "If we deal falsely with our God," Winthrop continued, "and so cause him to withdraw his present help from us, . . . we (shall) be consumed out of the good land whither we are going." This Puritan feeling of lofty purpose and special responsibility under God was passed on to later generations of Americans and became an important part of the way Americans viewed themselves and their nation. Viewed positively, it helped bind together the great majority of Americans, despite differing backgrounds. Viewed from a more critical stance, it helped justify Indian removal and black enslavement, because in the minds of the European-descended majority, the "chosen people" consisted only of themselves.

The Rise of Revivalism

Beginning in the eighteenth century, many Protestants took part in a new development in religion, centered in North America and Britain, called "revivalism." In those days, "revival" meant the opposite of religious apathy or "deadness." It was said that there was a "revival of religion" in town if more people began attending worship services, sought advice about how to attain salvation, and gave up frivolous pastimes. But the most important sign of revival was a rapid series of new testimonies of the gift of saving faith. "God has worked in my heart, and I do believe that he has forgiven my sins, even mine, through the blood of his Son Jesus Christ". For many churches with Puritan roots, this was, as we saw, a necessary condition for church membership. Therefore "revival" meant a quick numerical growth for the churches.

For most people who cared about such things, it was the mysterious working of God that induced these revivals to come and go to various towns. After all, saving faith was his gift. No special measures could or should be adopted to stir up a revival. It was on this point that a great change occurred during the middle third of the 1700s. More and more people began to believe that ministers should preach in a special way to inspire the experience of saving faith. Hymns should be selected for their power to move the heart. Special revival services or "meetings" should be conducted in addition to regular worship gatherings. Indeed, every worship service should be a revival meeting, and some particularly gifted ministers should travel from place to place to lead revival meetings. Above all, an identifiable experience of conviction and saving faith should constitute the only true "conversion" to Christianity. Without this, people were "unconverted" or "unsaved," no matter how upstanding their lives were or how regular their performance of religious duties. In many people's minds, saving faith became less God's gift and more a voluntary decision. In any case, whatever the shadings of opinion on this question of predestination versus free will, revivals began to be conducted *as if* sinners could make voluntary decisions for Christ.

The cluster of beliefs and practices just described is known by the term "revivalism": the effort to produce revival, particularly the one-two experience of conviction and saving faith. During the 1720s and 1730s, a scattered series of revivals, especially among Congregationalists and Presbyterians in New England, New York, and New Jersey, set the stage for a climactic wave of religious excitement in the 1740s, called the Great Awakening. Although many men and women shaped the Awakening, its most famous figure was the English minister George Whitefield, whose eloquent preaching transformed these separate revivals into an intercolonial movement of great power.

For at least a century afterward, revivalism was the most vigorous, most successful, movement in American Protestantism. After the Great Awakening came three decades of revival activity in Virginia and other southern colonies. The period after the War for Independence was a rather quiet one, but the first forty years of the nineteenth century bustled with a variety of revivalist episodes beginning with the so-called Second Great Awakening in New England. During this great age of the frontier camp meetings, hundreds, even thousands, would gather for several days of revivalist preaching, praying, and singing. This period also saw the best work of Charles G. Finney. His revival meetings in the major towns of western New York established new patterns and techniques for revival campaigns in the cities. Later revivalists, such as Dwight Moody after the Civil War and Billy Graham after the Second World War, borrowed many of the methods invented by Finney. We should note, however, that even when revivalism was strongest, many Protestants were untouched by it, and others vigorously opposed it.

It is fair to say that after 1850 or thereabouts revivalism lost its dominance in Protestant practice, giving way to increasing use of alternative patterns. But it is still tremendously influential. Even today, countless Protestants believe that the revival model provides the only correct way of becoming a Christian, as well as the only hope for the growth of Christianity.

Religious Liberty

It is sometimes hard for us to realize from our current viewpoint that for most of its history Christianity existed in legal partnership with various governments. Beginning in the fourth century, the government enforced religious uniformity; there could be no dissenting Christian groups. (Jews, where tolerated, lived by special charters or by the whims of Christian rulers. Any other religious movements, such as the pre-Christian religions of various lands, could exist only in secret.) This was true not only in Catholic and

Orthodox lands, but also in Protestant territories in the sixteenth and seventeenth centuries.

Therefore, many of the colonists in North America duplicated these established systems of religious uniformity, enforced by the colonial governments similar to those in Europe. In Virginia, and the other colonies, and in New York, the Church of England was the "established," official religion. In most New England colonies, Congregationalism was the established religion. The intention of this coalition of church and state was to tolerate no other religions on their soil. People were imprisoned, banished, or, on rare occasions, executed, for publicly proclaiming other forms of Christianity; religious offenses, such as irreverently speaking God's name, were punishable by law; and the government supported the church by tax revenue.

Some of the colonial governments were never strong enough to enforce their religious laws consistently. Furthermore, there were cases where new immigrants were needed so desperately that people were allowed to settle despite their dissenting religions. Such were the Scotch-Irish Presbyterians in Virginia and North Carolina, who were permitted to form a buffer in the western mountains between the coastal Anglicans and the Indians. Other economic and political reasons made it convenient to tolerate dissenters. For instance, in 1689 Britain changed its religious policy by means of the Act of Toleration. The newly tolerant British pressed the overseas colonies to change their policies too. Gradually they did so.

Thus, by the time of the Revolution the colonies that had started out trying to enforce religious uniformity were actually compelled to administer various plans of religious toleration. It is important to realize that "toleration" was a middle ground policy somewhere between religious uniformity and religious liberty. There was still an established religion, but certain dissenting groups could worship unmolested, often under a system where ministers and church buildings were licensed by the government. However, the government normally continued to discriminate against dissenters in other ways, such as barring them from public office and taxing them to support the established church. The government also specified which groups were eligible for this limited program of toleration, which normally consisted only of Protestant groups and not even all of those, although Maryland tolerated Catholics.

On the threshold of nationhood, most of the colonies had experienced a history of enforced conformity transformed into toleration, under which tens of thousands of dissenters lived in peace. In addition, four colonies had longstanding policies of religious liberty. In Rhode Island, Pennsylvania, Delaware, and New Jersey, governments did not regulate religion at all. Naturally, these places became havens for large numbers of the more radical Protestant groups and a scattering of Catholics and Jews as well. Such was the situation facing the Constitutional Convention in 1787. On the practical side, it was impossible to choose one religious group to be favored over the others. There were several powerful ones, but no single one was in the majority. On the theoretical side, most people agreed by this time that having an official religion was not good for the government or for the churches. So the Constitution makers wrote the government out of the business of regulating religion: no one could be barred from office on account of religion (Article Six); and Congress could not favor one religion over another or restrict the free exercise of religion (First Amendment). The United States thus became the first nation to view all religious groups as voluntary associations freely competing for members without support or hindrance from government.

The Protestant Mainstream: The Golden Age

As was suggested earlier, we should not draw any hasty conclusions about the fact that there are so many Protestant denominations. Although there were and are hard-fought issues between Protestants, there is also a history of harmony and cooperation. During the years from 1800 to 1860, the beliefs, purposes, and methods of most Protestants were unified to the point that some scholars speak of America in that period as a kind of "Protestant Empire." Although not officially connected with the government, Protestants thought of America as a Protestant nation. They believed that to be a loyal American one had to be Protestant, a conviction which was not completely abandoned until very recent times. Conversely, the idea of a Protestant nation also meant that Protestants felt responsible for improving the religious and moral life of the whole nation. This was consistent with the Puritan idea, noted earlier, of a "chosen people" with special privileges and special responsibilities. There are different opinions of how well Protestants lived up to their self-imposed responsibility, but everyone agrees that they tried hard.

One of the clear successes was in following the westward-moving population. When the Declaration of

Independence was signed in 1776, the population of the infant nation was about 2.5 million, nearly all living in the thirteen states east of the Appalachian chain. Notably, this was the low point of religious affiliation *per capita* in this country's colonial and national history. About one American in fifteen was a church member. Eighty years later, there were ten times as many people, living in thirty states and eight territories from coast to coast. Such rapid expansion was a threat to established eastern institutions, including the churches. The danger was that the ministers might not be able to move as fast as the covered wagons, leaving the frontier people without the leadership necessary to maintain their religious feeling and practice. It was true that the oldest denominations, the Congregationalists and Episcopalians[1], were unable to respond quickly to the challenge of the west. But the newer denominations could do so: Baptists, Methodists, and (less successfully) Presbyterians. The result was that the western regions became as staunchly Protestant as the original thirteen states. In fact, the percentage of church members in the total American population more than doubled in the eighty year period.

Success for the Baptists and Methodists in converting and organizing the rural West was the result of several techniques. Both churches were committed to revivalist methods; their teaching was easy to explain; the worship services were direct and stimulating. But most important of all, the two groups developed patterns of leadership that guaranteed that ministers could move as fast as the population. Most Baptist frontier ministers in those days were farmers, who received no pay for their church duties. Ordination was granted from the congregation. They had only to demonstrate to their neighbors that they had the necessary gifts from God to be a minister. In this way, Baptists carried their own ministers with them as rapidly as they moved westward.

Equally adaptable to the frontier was the Methodist ministry, although it was organized differently from the Baptist ministry. Instead of being "one of the people," locally elected and ordained as a Baptist minister was, the Methodist minister was recruited by other ministers and, after a trial period, ordained by a bishop. Usually unmarried, the Methodist minister carried most of his belongings in his saddlebags and went wherever the

---

1. The Protestant Episcopal Church was formed after the Revolution from the depleted membership of the Church of England. Thus, the Episcopalians are American Anglicans.

bishop sent him. Often his assignment would be a frontier "circuit" made up of widely separated cabins, trading posts, and other humble spots. It might take as long as six weeks just to ride around the whole circuit, preaching, instructing, and baptizing. And then he started a round again. After a year, he was moved somewhere else, leaving his former circuit in the hands of one or more other ministers. After a few years of this method, every point on that wilderness circuit had become a thriving Methodist congregation.

However, the leaders of the Protestant Empire were interested in more than enrolling church members and saving souls for heaven. They also wanted to improve the people's behavior. As we learned, the Puritans forged a tight link between religious faith and daily life. Now the Protestants of the nineteenth century, thinking of themselves as the heirs of the Puritan tradition, also cited religious reasons for moral reform. For one thing, they believed that conversion should be followed by moral improvement (or, as they called it, "holiness"), but some believers seemed to be lagging in this regard. They also believed that God was moving the whole nation (and world) toward the age of righteousness and the end of all evil, and that their energetic action could hasten that day.

Subscribers to these beliefs created an amazing organizational network with strong grass roots support for a variety of moral reform projects. The typical organization was a local "society," one of thousands, represented in parallel state and national societies. For instance, the American Temperance Society, formed in 1826, was supported by hundreds of local temperance societies. As a way of organizing for benevolent and reform activities, voluntary societies had many advantages. They were bands of individuals who did not have to wait for approval from church assemblies. They could gather like-minded people from several competing denominations with a minimum of fuss. By successfully soliciting funds in offices, homes, lecture halls, and the churches of pastors friendly to their cause, they bypassed the restrictions of church treasuries. Above all they could concentrate their energy on a single task or problem. Favorite causes included reducing or eliminating the use of alcohol, suppressing prostitution and rescuing prostitutes, and prohibiting Sunday ("Sabbath") work and public amusements. Other societies were devoted to distributing free Bibles and religious tracts, establishing Sunday schools, creating academies and colleges, and a variety of other causes of humanitarian or educational reform.

From the vantage point of a later time, we can see both

strengths and weaknesses in the Protestant reform movement. On the one hand, it managed to achieve a remarkable consensus about what constitutes acceptable behavior, thus creating a basis for civic harmony in the face of severe stresses within American society. Furthermore, Protestant groups for a time provided most of the secondary education in the western regions. For a longer time, they accounted for most of the nation's private colleges and universities. Mainstream Protestants had a role in such humanitarian movements as prison reform, abolition of war, and abolition of slavery. But it must be admitted that these collective ills of society were combatted mainly by people outside of the mainstream, such as Quakers in the case of the peace movement. Indeed, it has been observed that the mainstream reformers usually limited their action to the vices of individuals. Ignored by their crusading zeal were the more complicated agonies of a growing nation. Generally, they were unable to speak sensibly about the poverty that grew along with new factories and production-oriented agriculture. Admitting the existence of "poor but honest" persons, they by and large viewed poverty as the result of the vices of poor people. Therefore their charity (in both senses of the word) tended to be meager and condescending.

In the matter of the enslavement of blacks, we can see most clearly the limitations of the Protestant reform movement. Originating in the "unthinking decision" of the seventeenth century, slavery in the nineteenth century was fully woven into the thinking of most Americans, whether slaveholders or not. Only a few, small churches and sects had rules against members' owning slaves; all of the large and fast-growing denominations had thousands of slaveholding members. In other words, for the great majority of Protestants, North and South, slaveholding was not a sin, as drunkenness and adultery were sins. Slavery was variously described by southern Protestants as a necessary evil or a positive good. After 1831, no discussion of abolition was tolerated. In the North, there were vestiges of slavery, but most blacks were legally free, while being restricted by laws applying only to them. Most northerners, including most white Protestants, agreed that blacks were not suited for the privileges and responsibilities of citizenship; that free blacks should be carefully controlled by law and custom; and that slaves should remain slaves or perhaps be emancipated very, very slowly.

With the formation of the American Antislavery Society in 1833, a national abolitionist movement was born. By and large, the churches did not support abolitionism.

For this reason, many abolitionist leaders, such as William Lloyd Garrison, bitterly criticized the churches and refused to be church members. At the same time, there were pockets of church-oriented abolitionists, notably in New England and Ohio. Such people as Theodore Dwight Weld formed embattled minorities within the major denominations. They did not give up their Protestant credentials nor their religious arguments against slavery. Nevertheless, looking back to the heyday of abolitionism, it would be hard for Protestants to take credit for leading the movement. Failure on this issue weakened the claim of Protestantism to being a nation's conscience. The Civil War, which threw American Protestants against each other, marked the end — or the beginning of the end — of the one time Protestant Empire.

Liberal Protestantism: The Mainstream Divides

Up to the 1870s, it is useful to speak of a principal type of American Protestantism that created broad agreement on religious and moral matters and claimed the allegiance (at least informally) of a majority of the nation's people. We have already seen the main terms of the agreement: the corruption of human nature by sin, saving faith in Christ as the cure for sin and the gateway to salvation and church life, the Bible as the infallible Word of God, America as a divinely guided nation, righteousness linked with prosperity and vice linked with poverty, and finally the moral and social superiority of Protestants and Catholics and of whites over blacks.

It should be observed that even in the golden years of the Protestant Empire there were Protestants who separated themselves from the consensus just described: Amish and Mennonites, whose separated communities were intended to deny that America or any other nation could be "Christian"; certain "high church" Lutherans and Episcopalians, who thought the mainstreamers had altered Christianity to suit the mood of the masses; Mormons, whose belief in special revelations to Joseph Smith and a succession of living prophets set them apart from the mainstream; Adventists, who emphasized the second coming of Christ; Unitarians, who denied orthodox views of the nature of Christ; and Universalists, who denied eternal damnation. This is only a fractional list. Dissent was vigorous, and "cults" and "sects" abounded. Yet the consensus also grew and prospered, showing amazing power and imagination in appealing to diverse sorts of people. For instance, it was based on English-speaking groups, yet was successful in crossing language barriers and integrating large numbers of Germans and Scandinavians into the mainstream. So even though there were dissenting voices, the mainstream ran broad and deep up to the Civil War and beyond.

Beginning in the 1870s, however, we can see the development of a different Protestant type, usually called liberalism. It had different ideas about human nature, the authority of the Bible, and how people became Christians. We are justified in thinking of the rise of liberal Protestantism as a split in the mainstream rather than another dissenting voice. For one thing, liberalism had a mainstream mentality; its proponents thought of themselves as reinterpreting Christianity for modern America. Their power base consisted of many influential urban congregations of the time. Major seminaries and universities became centers of liberal thought. Furthermore the liberal version of Christian faith did not aim to be elitist or exclusive, and it was not hard for people to understand. It grew and prospered, most notably in the cities and larger towns of the North. By the time of the First World War, perhaps half of all Protestants could be counted in the liberal camp, with most others maintaining allegiance to the conservative-revivalist type.

No movement of this importance begins suddenly. Many of the elements that were blended into the liberal movement existed earlier, such as the emphasis on "reason" in religion and the belief of a minority of Protestants that people were basically good rather than innately corrupt. Yet more was required to transform scattered dissent into a broad and durable movement such as liberalism became. That "more" necessary for a definable split came to America in the form of exposure to Charles Darwin's theory of evolution by natural selection and to new German developments in the historical study of the Bible. These two clusters of ideas created a crisis of faith for so many people that a major rethinking of Christian teaching was required. Protestant liberalism was born.

Darwin published *The Origin of Species* in 1859, but it was not well known among scientists in the United States until ten years later. Although most of them were more or less orthodox Protestants, the general response in the scientific community was positive, even enthusiastic. Evolution became the reigning idea of biology (and of much philosophy and social science as well), apparently tying together observations by many researchers. The overarching theory was simply that all presently existing species, both animals and plants, developed out of older and simpler species, which no longer exist. The earliest organisms were something like the simplest one-cell organisms that exist today. Darwin's contribution was to compile a lot of data in support of the evolutionary idea generally and to identify "natural selection" as the mechanism for changing one species into another (or several other) species. Furthermore, Darwin's *The Descent of Man* (1871) clearly stated that human beings were the result of the same evolutionary process that produced other species.

The theory assaulted traditional Christian thought patterns on three points. First, it pictured the origin of humans as a gradual emergence from animal ancestors rather than a sudden creative act by a transcendental being. In doing so, it deprived people of a convenient way to see themselves as unique among God's creatures. Second, by attributing evolution to the machine-like process called natural selection, Darwin made it hard for people to imagine how God fit into the story of the development of earth's inhabitants. Natural selection evoked images of "the survival of the fittest" and "nature red in tooth and claw," rather than the wise plan of a loving God. Third, Darwin's "story" of life's development was not the same as the Bible's story, which Christians assumed covered the same events. Therefore, Darwin seemed to attack the authority of the Bible.

Problems over these matters, especially the authority of the Bible, were further aggravated by ideas that had nothing to do with Darwin. These ideas arose from new and exciting ways of studying history, including the notion that the only way to understand the present is to examine the past in great detail. It is hard for most readers now to imagine the enthusiasm that the idea of "history" aroused among the reading public in the nineteenth century. Among the several ways that historical studies affected religion, the most important was the scholarly study of the Bible. Historians set about examining the Bible, using the same methods they used in dealing with historical documents. They searched out questions of authorship, dates, literary form, and parallels with other ancient literature. For instance, one famous German scholar concluded that the Bible's first five books (the Pentateuch or Books of Moses) were composed by several authors (one of whom might have been Moses) over a period of several centuries. While such conclusions were not intended as a comment on the authority of the Bible, their effect was to emphasize the human circumstances of scripture writing, thus diminishing the perception of the Bible as an infallible message from God.

It is not surprising that American Protestantism produced many opponents of evolutionary theory and modern Biblical scholarship. Opposition is still very much alive today among Protestants who call themselves "evangelicals." What is remarkable is that a century ago Protestants also put forth many articulate and convincing *proponents* of those same ideas. Those early liberals and the growing numbers who followed them saw evolutionary and historical ideas as the occasion for a new style of Christianity for a new day. Interpreting Darwin in a context of high optimism, they insisted that evolution is controlled by God and that human beings are his grandest achievement. For them, evolution was God's way of working out his loving plan for the world. Evolution meant progress, and progress meant hope. And modern Biblical scholarship merely showed evolution in another sphere, the sphere of religious ideas, leading up to Jesus Christ, who was the highest revelation of God's desire for humanity. Thus, although the Bible was not infallible, it did have unsurpassed authority, for it revealed the son of God, Jesus Christ.

Ideas of evolution-development-growth also influenced liberals' thinking in the matter of how the individual acquires Christian faith and virtue. They had no use for revival techniques, and denied the necessity of an identifiable conversion experience. Instead they placed a new emphasis on Christian education and the gradual transformation of the individual from childhood to Christian maturity. By example and instruction, the individual would be led in easy stages to the fullness of Christian life.

Growing in popularity between the Civil War and the First World War, liberalism inspired a strong reaction from the more traditional Protestants. The conservative leaders defended their views by carefully defining those doctrines they believed were "fundamental" to Christian faith, particularly human corruption or depravity, the Godhood or deity of Christ, and the inerrancy or infallibility of the Bible. Because they stressed these and other fundamentals, they often called themselves Fundamentalists. Their struggle against the liberals was especially intense in the teens and twenties of this century. The result was a deep and lasting cleavage within the Protestant mainstream. The conservative-Fundamentalist-"evangelical" side emphasized the inerrancy of the Bible and the need for a personal conversion to Christ. The liberal-modernist-"progressive" side emphasized harmony with modern ideas of science and history, as well as gradual growth toward Christian ideals. Despite their differences, the liberals and conservatives were united in moral values, patriotism, and racial views.

Empire's End

The years between the Civil War and the First World War saw the decline of Protestant influence and consensus. We have already seen two of the reasons for this. The first was the Civil War itself, which has been characterized as a double holy war. That is, people with identical assumptions about God and country were fighting each other. Both sides were deeply convinced that God was supporting their cause. The bitterness engendered by sectionalism and warfare produced lasting divisions within church bodies. For instance, the Methodists were divided along sectional lines from 1844 until 1939. After the war, Protestants north and south blamed each other for tearing the churches apart and treasured the belief that the other side had departed from the true faith.

In addition to sectional division, we have seen how the Protestant mainstream split into conservative and liberal tendencies, neither speaking for a majority on most issues. There also seemed to be an increase in the number of dissenting voices. The mass of black people, newly freed, certainly did not blend with the organizations and concerns of white Protestants. Their distinctive institutions will be examined in the next chapter. Among whites, there were new groups emphasizing stricter standards of morality ("holiness" groups such as the Nazarenes), special "gifts" of the Holy Spirit (Pentecostal groups), and mental healing (Christian Science). These concerns could no longer be held within the denominations of the Protestant Empire, and their departure hastened its end.

A third reason for Protestant decline between the Civil War and the First World War was related to the growth of American industry and the number of industrial workers. This was the time of great unrest among the industrial labor force. In an atmosphere of periodic depression and oppressive working conditions, the nation witnessed a series of strikes, beginning with the railroad strike of 1877, which included pitched battles between workers and police (including private security forces, national guard, and federal troops). By and large, Protestants found their strength among farmers and business people. They were suspicious of industrial workers as a group, partly because so many of them were foreign-born and Catholic. Protestant leaders in the main, both conservative and liberal, sided with employers against workers. However, in the eighties and nineties, some leaders representing a minority of the liberal movement began defending the workers and urging improvement of their wages and working conditions. This movement emphasizing the needs of the poor, especially urban workers, was called the Social Gospel. Washington Gladden, a Congregational minister in Columbus, was one of the best known Social Gospel leaders. Differences between employer-oriented Protestants and the worker-oriented Social Gospelers further disrupted Protestant harmony.

Another problem for Protestants was the immigration of large numbers of Catholics and smaller contingents of Jews and Eastern Orthodox Christians. As the non-Protestant segment grew toward thirty percent of the American population, many Protestants were genuinely afraid that democratic institutions were in danger. These fears contributed to efforts to restrain the political power of the newcomers, which failed, and a campaign to restrict immigration, which triumphed in 1921 and 1924. Protestants had to adjust to the fact that a third of the population neither practiced Protestant religion nor respected it as the conscience of the nation.

Perhaps the hardest blow to Protestant confidence and power, however, was World War I (1914-1918). In the decades before the war, many Protestants shared the current middle-class optimism; they believed that the world was on the verge of a new era of peace, justice, and prosperity. Idealistic college students by the hundreds became missionaries in Asia and Africa. Some envisioned a worldwide Christian civilization just around the corner. Then Europe burst into flames. America entered the "war to end all wars," which dragged along to a disillusioning end. Idealism turned to dismay, and the Protestant vision of a bright new world lost its credibility. Protestant self-confidence faltered; church attendance and financial support declined; disputes between liberals and conservatives became more bitter and divisive.

Yet Protestantism retained its capacity to engage the lives of millions of people at the deepest personal level. It also provided the context for a good deal of social action and comment from both right and left sides of the political spectrum. But it had lost its capacity to unite a nation, to assemble a consensus around common patterns of religious behavior and moral value. There was no more Protestant Empire.

Depression, War, Recovery

Disillusion and decline were accented by the Great Depression. Many churches were forced to devote all their energy to merely keeping the doors open. Paying the bills and helping people cope with poverty and loss of self-esteem, there were many quiet acts of heroism. There could be little pursuit of high ideals on a grand scale. The Second World War, which the United States entered in December 1941, relieved people's money problems but created anxieties and family problems that effectively restrained the development of the churches.

The postwar period, however, was a time of expanding religious activity. Historians speak of the "religious revival" or the "surge of piety" of the fifties and early sixties. The portion of Americans affiliated with religious organizations increased from forty-three percent in 1920 to a peak of sixty-nine percent in 1960 before it began declining. Along with the growth in membership came an increase in attendance at religious services and in the construction of church buildings. In the peak year of 1960, Americans spent over a billion dollars to build houses of worship. All religious groups shared in this expansion, but Protestantism, which was already the natural preference of two thirds of the nation, prospered the most.

Many reasons can account for this surge of piety in American life. One was that the churches were family-oriented institutions in an increasingly mobile society where families were having a tough time. Churches provided a sense of belonging to people on the move. Also, in those days of Cold War confrontation with the Soviet Union, there was a connection between being a good American and being religious, especially since the enemies were "godless Communists." Futhermore, several types of religious renewal converged in this period to swell the growth: the resurgence of conservative Protestant revivalism, a new interest in religious education to serve the postwar "baby boom," and, in addition, the Protestant ecumenical movement.

The word "ecumenical" refers to efforts to unite and reform the whole Church. In recent history, it applies to two separate movements: a Catholic effort in the sixties and a Protestant and Eastern Orthodox movement which had its postwar beginning in the first general assembly of the World Council of Churches in Amsterdam in 1948. Americans became more aware of the movement through their own National Council of Churches and through the convention of the second assembly of the World Council of Churches in Evanston, Illinois, in 1954.

Among the results of the ecumenical movement have been friendlier relations between Protestant and Eastern Orthodox churches. In this country, members of the various Orthodox churches — especially Greek, Romanian, Ukrainian, and Russian — arrived after the Civil War in the same migration from eastern and southern Europe that brought so many Catholics and Jews. Today about 1.5 percent of Americans are Orthodox Christians. It was the ecumenical movement that provided a forum for Protestants and Orthodox to discuss their similarities and differences. The movement led to various forms of Protestant inter-church cooperation and to the uniting of some Protestant groups into new and larger denominations. In one noteworthy case an old denominational label virtually disappeared as most Congregational churches united with another body in 1957 to form the United Church of Christ.

White Protestantism in Crisis

The twenty years after 1960 brought such change and uncertainty to American society — racial struggle, the Indo-China War, Watergate, economic crisis, and political demoralization — that it was no longer possible to speak of America's old majority faith in terms of recovery or renewal. Of course, these disturbing events affected others in addition to white Protestants, but the latter were affected to a greater degree because they had, so to speak, more to lose.

One way to perceive this loss is to remember the history of Protestant predominance in this country. Even after the development of a large Catholic minority and a smaller Jewish one, two-thirds of all Americans identified themselves as Protestants. Up to 1960, these people still had a comforting feeling that this was their country and that other groups were moving toward conformity with their standards. Now consider how their situation changed.

The election of the first Catholic president in 1960 was a potent symbol of the end of the Protestant era. However, much more threatening was the rise of a religiously based black civil rights movement. Many whites saw for the first time that black Protestants were a distinctive and self-directing group, rather than an inferior echo of white

Protestantism. Although some whites allied themselves with the black movement, there were others who viewed the movement as an ungrateful withdrawal from the Protestant consensus.

The Vietnam War marked an equal or greater disruption among Protestants. As anti-war sentiment grew during the late sixties, Protestants were involved on both sides of the debate. Congregations and denominations engaged in bitter internal struggles. Many younger Protestants who were involved in anti-war activities became convinced that traditional religion was hostile to their values. They explored religious alternatives, such as Asian religions and occult traditions. Even those who stayed in touch with Protestantism often adopted a strongly anti-intellectual position. This was one of the characteristics of the so-called Jesus movement, in which some features of conservative Protestantism were combined with such features of the youth culture as distinctive dress and rock-style music. The movement consisted mostly of informal groups that were unrelated to established religious organizations.

As Protestantism enters the 1980s, many of the faithful are discouraged while others believe that the troubled times offer new opportunities for serious Christians. Certainly in the centuries before 1607 Protestantism on this continent has shown a remarkable capacity to respond to crisis, to stir people's deepest feelings, and to reflect the nation's changing moods.

Selected People and Events

1607 The founding of Jamestown, Virginia, marking the beginning of continuous British settlement in North America, and the beginning of the Church of England in America.

1620 Arrival of the Pilgrims (a Puritan group) in Plymouth, New England, later absorbed into Massachusetts.

1626 New Netherland (later New York) organized as a Dutch colony. The beginning of the Dutch Reformed Church in North America.

1630 Beginning of a decade of heavy Puritan (Congregationalist) immigration to Massachusetts and Connecticut.

1636 Roger Williams (1604?-1684), Puritan pioneer of religious liberty, established Providence (Rhode Island).

1637 Anne Hutchinson (1591-1643), Puritan lay theologian, was banished from Massachusetts after theological and political controversy, and settled in Rhode Island.

1710 Beginning of several decades of heavy Scotch-Irish (Presbyterian) and German (Lutheran, Reformed, etc.) immigration to America.

1734 Revival in Northampton, Massachusetts, under the brilliant Congregationalist minister Jonathan Edwards (1703-1758); the prelude to the Great Awakening.

1755 Shubal Stearns (1706-1771) established a Baptist church at Sandy Creek, North Carolina. The beginning of rapid Baptist growth in the South after decades of weak reponse is part of the southern Great Awakening.

1784 The organization of the Methodist Episcopal Church, the main body of American Methodists, with Francis Asbury (1745-1816) as its first bishop.

1789 Inauguration of the first national administration under the Constitution and the Bill of Rights. The beginning of religious liberty at the national level.

1801 The Cane Ridge revival, Bourbon County, Kentucky. One of the first of the frontier camp meetings, marking the beginning of "The Great Revival of the West."

1821 The beginning of the career of Charles Grandison Finney (1792-1875), the most famous traveling revivalist of his time, and the pioneer of techniques of urban mass evangelism.

1837 Elijah Lovejoy, a church-oriented abolitionist, is murdered while defending his printing press from a pro-slavery mob in Alton, Illinois. This event increased the intensity of the abolitionist movement.

1852 The publication of *Uncle Tom's Cabin*, an extremely influential anti-slavery novel by Harriet Beecher Stowe (1811-1896), a church-oriented abolitionist.

1860 Ellen Gould White (1827-1915), the "Adventist Prophetess," organized the Seventh-Day Adventist Church.

1861 Julia Ward Howe wrote "The Battle Hymn of the Republic," which depicted Union soldiers as the army of God. Confederates held identical sentiments about their army.

1870 The beginning of a large Scandinavian immigration. The mostly Lutheran group made up the last major Protestant ethnic group to arrive in the United States.

1875 Mary Baker Eddy (1821-1910) held the first public Christian Science service and published the first edition of *Science and Health.*

1875 The first American revival campaigns of Dwight Moody (1837-1899), the most famous professional evangelist of the period.

1892 Lyman Abbott (1835-1922), liberal minister of an in-influential congregation in Brooklyn, published *The Evolution of Christianity*, an important example of the use of evolutionary theory in popular theology.

1907 The publication of *Christianity and the Social Crisis* by Walter Rauschenbusch (1861-1918), a classic statement of the Social Gospel.

1908 Founding of the Federal Council of Churches, which was reorganized in 1950 as the National Council of Churches. By 1960, included several Eastern Orthodox groups, thus ceasing to be exclusively Protestant.

1910 Publication of the first issue of *The Fundamentals*, a series of twelve booklets by conservative theologians intended to help ministers and others to combat liberalism.

1917 Congress passed the Eighteenth Amendment, prohibiting alcoholic beverages, representing the last successful national Protestant crusade, uniting conservatives and liberals alike. Repealed in 1933.

1924 A restrictive immigration bill was passed, partly in response to a Protestant fear of a Catholic-Jewish-Bolshevik takeover. Immigration from eastern and southern Europe was reduced to a trickle, and the Protestant constituency was stabilized at about two-thirds of the American population.

1932 Publication of Reinhold Neibuhr's (1862-1970) *Moral Man and Immoral Society*, which questioned the social views of both liberal and conservative Protestants. Neibuhr and his brother, H. Richard Neibuhr, helped to create a third theological alternative for Protestants, called "neo-orthodoxy", which was also important in the postwar years.

1941 The National Association of Evangelicals was founded by moderate conservatives to counteract the moderate liberalism of the Federal (later National) Council of Churches.

1949 Billy Graham (b. 1918) gained national fame while leading a revival meeting in Los Angeles. Most important professional evangelist of the last thirty years, Graham is credited with giving new popularity to the revivalist tradition and to conservative Protestantism generally.

1953 The Presbyterian General Council, opposing the anti-Communist "investigations" of Sen. Joseph McCarthy, stated that "detestation of Communism" was becoming a dangerous "new form of idolatry." By contrast, many Protestants supported McCarthy.

1962 The first meeting of the Consultation on Church Union, a continuing attempt by several major Protestant denominations to work out a plan of union. An example of the ecumenical movement.

1965 The major escalation of the Vietnam War, heralding years of crisis and division in the churches.

1976 General Convention of the Episcopal Church voted to admit women to the priesthood.

CHAPTER FOUR

Black Religion: The Vision of Freedom

Africans began arriving in North America in 1619, not as immigrants but as captives. Because the needs and hopes of black people in America were so different from those of whites, it is not surprising that African-descended people developed distinctive religious forms. Black religion has been closely tied to the black struggle for survival, dignity, and freedom. In this respect black religion resembles Indian religion, for both groups have been victims of white goals and strategies. Despite important differences, their shared experience includes not only massive physical abuse but spiritual abuse as well: being defined by the dominant culture as inferior, degenerate, and dangerous. Religion is relevant to all aspects of life, but it is especially potent in battling that kind of spiritual assault.

Slavery in North America

Winthrop Jordan referred to the introduction of

African slavery into North America as "the unthinking decision." The first British settlements in Virginia and New England were not planned with slavery in mind. However, when wage labor, white servitude, and Indian slavery failed to provide sufficient labor, the colonists began imitating their Spanish enemies by purchasing Africans as slaves. By 1700, slavery was well established in law and practice in all the British colonies. At the time of the Revolution one-fifth of the inhabitants of the new nation were Africans by birth or descent. Ninety percent of the blacks were enslaved, while the free minority were subject to restrictions that applied only to them or to blacks and Indians together.

Slavery in the British colonies began as part of a larger European movement. The African slave trade, originated by the Portuguese in 1441, was in full swing in the sixteenth century, as Spain and Portugal transported thousands of captives to labor in the New World colonies. Holland, France, and Britain joined in later. In the four centuries of the Atlantic slave trade, ten million people were torn from their African homeland. Of those who survived the voyage, the great majority landed in South America and the Caribbean islands. About 5 percent landed within the present boundaries of the United States.

Because all the slave-trading nations were Christian powers, either Catholic or Protestant, it is helpful to know something of the historic relationship between slavery and Christianity. The institution of slavery had existed for thousands of years, flourishing in societies connected with every major religion. It was part of the Roman Empire, in which Christianity arose, and therefore became part of Christian society. Both slaves and owners were baptized into the early church and were urged to regard each other as brothers and sisters in Christ, and perhaps they were sometimes able to do so. However, as time went on and Christianity became the official religion of the Roman Empire and then of the nations of Europe, the church developed rigid structures of law and theology to regulate slavery. These teachings tried to protect simultaneously the slave's humanity and the owner's property rights, but it was always easier to enforce the slave's obligations than the master's. Thus, in addition to the usual burdens of servitude, Christian slaves had to labor under the accusation of sin if they did not render full obedience to their owners. Trying to run away, for instance, brought not only harsh earthly penalties upon slaves but also threatened to exclude them from heaven. In general, then, the Christian religion was as comfortable with slavery as any other religion was. After western Christendom split in the sixteenth century, both Protestants and Catholics remained united in their teaching about slavery. Whether the traders were Spanish Catholics or British Protestants, no voice was raised to oppose the kidnapping and enslavement of Africans until late in the seventeenth century.

In the British colonies nearly all whites agreed that Africans were destined by God to be slaves of white people. Various biblical arguments were used to demonstrate this but the colonists did not require much proof. Clergymen and congregations became involved in the growth of slavery in a number of ways, but chiefly by regarding it as normal for church members to buy, sell, and use other human beings as personal property. The first people to declare that Christians should not be slaveholders were certain members of the Society of Friends, a Protestant group whose members are often called Quakers. In 1675, William Edmundson, an Irish Quaker traveling in the colonies, urged slaveholding Friends to free their slaves. In 1688, Quakers in Germantown, Pennsylvania, declared that slavery was un-Christian, because it violated Christ's Golden Rule. No one wants to be treated as a slave, they declared, and therefore no Christian should hold anyone as a slave.

For a long time, such protests were ignored or suppressed, even within the Society of Friends, but eventually the Quakers became known for their anti-slavery convictions. After the Revolution they provided a nucleus for other Christians of similar mind. In the nineteenth century, such people, using religious arguments against slavery, contributed to the abolitionist movement, which was one of the causes of the Civil War, which became the occasion for ending slavery. Meanwhile most Christians, north and south, either used religious arguments to justify slavery or else declared that slavery was not a religious issue and should be left alone. They reserved their harsh words for abolitionists and blacks rather than slaveholders. Thus, although there was a dissenting white minority, Christianity was normally interpreted as permitting, and sometimes as encouraging, the enslavement of Africans.

It is important to remember this background while following the development of black religion in America. When blacks began looking positively at the Christian religion, they could not accept the white interpretation that supported their enslavement. What many of them accepted was a vision of Christ the Liberator, the divine enemy of slavery. Before considering that development, however, it is necessary to look at the religion that the captives brought from Africa.

African Traditional Religion

What was the religious situation of the nearly half-million Africans who arrived in North America during the years of the Atlantic slave trade? A few, having come by way of Spanish or Portuguese colonies, were Roman Catholics or at least had been baptized in that faith. A larger number were Muslims, as their Arabic names testify. Islam was well established in some west African lands, though often as the religion only of the upper classes. Some ex-slaves as late as the 1930s remembered seeing grandfathers reciting prayers in the Muslim way. But the bulk of captive Africans practiced the traditional religions of Africa, resembling in many ways the religions of American Indians, as well as the ancient religions of Greece, Babylonia, and Egypt.

There are two problems in describing the religion that Africans brought to this country. The first is the scarcity of reliable reports from the days of the slave trade. Careful, sympathetic reporting is pretty much a product of the twentieth century. However, there is some evidence that recent religious beliefs and practices resemble those of the past in many important ways, so that we can describe the African heritage by combining recent studies with available historical testimony. The second problem is that there were and are many African religions, and not just one. Among different kingdoms, tribes, and clans, there were thousands of small variations and dozens of major ones. The problem is somewhat simplified by looking only at the western regions of the continent, from which most New World blacks were taken. Then the black Old World heritage can be described by identifying the religious elements common to all the societies from which American blacks are descended.

Leonard E. Barrett (*Soul-Force,* 17) suggests that if there were such a thing as an African religious creed, it would look something like this.

> *I believe in a supreme being who creates all things, and in lesser deities, spirits and powers who guard and control the universe, I believe in the ancestors, who guard and protect their descendants. I believe in the efficacy of sacrifice and the power of magic, good and evil; and I believe in the fullness of life here and now.*

This imaginary creed serves as a guide to the common elements of the religions of western Africa during the years of the slave trade.

The High God and Other Deities. Apparently all the relevant African societies believed in a High God or Supreme Being. This deity was spoken of as the source and preserver of all things. He was above the day-to-day affairs of human beings and therefore had no shrines and received no sacrifices. In some societies he was scarcely mentioned, while in others people made spontaneous appeals to him. Ranged around and beneath the High God were many other deities, major and minor. These were sometimes viewed as personified attributes of the High God, sometimes as his assistants, and sometimes as virtually independent of him. Each of these deities had a particular function or combination of functions. These functions may relate to aspects of nature, as crops or iron, or to aspects of group life, as overseeing oaths or empowering warriors. In this way dozens or hundreds of deities maintained all of the functions of the universe. Each of the major deities had one or more shrines and priests, through which people could offer worship. The most important form of worship consisted of various rituals of sacrifice, in which animals or other valuable gifts were offered. Many of these sacrifices were great public events carefully scheduled according to a calendar of rituals. At other times individuals or families would offer sacrifices in behest of private needs.

Ancestors and Other Spirits. As with American Indians, the African world was alive with spirits. Some were indistinguishable from minor deities, such as animals, trees, rivers, rocks, and swamps. Others were associated with humans, both the ones we would call living and those we would call dead. Certain dead spirits became harmful ghosts, and people took careful measures to avoid or repulse them. Others were the spirits of recent generations of one's own family and clan. These were the friendly ancestor spirits, often called the "living dead" (not to be confused with the evil vampire spirits of European folklore). The living dead were regarded as powerful helpers and protectors of their living ancestors. Therefore religious ceremonies were directed toward the ancestor spirits, although not the same kind of ceremonies as those addressed to deities.

Power and Magic. The African idea of Sacred Power was not limited to deities and spirits. There was also that pervasive non-personal power, called *mana* in Chapter Two and specifically known by dozens of African terms. It was believed that deities and spirits had this power but that they were not the only ones who could control it. Various kinds of experts or specialists could manipulate it with magical procedures, for either good or ill. Thus healing power and hurting power were closely related. One very important type of magic was divination, which consisted of various ways of revealing hidden information. Each African society had one or more kinds of diviners. Their power was believed to come from a spirit or deity, but their techniques did not require worship ceremonies and so are classified as magic. Each type of diviner operated in a particular way, involving a store of traditional wisdom and a supernatural technique for selecting the portion of traditional wisdom that should be applied to the client's problem. Most African diviners were thought of as problem-solvers, who provided their clients with a framework for confident decision-making in times of crisis.

These, then, were the broad features of an African world-view: a universe united under a High God and supervised in every detail by deities and spirits; close family ties that extended beyond the grave; solemn and potent ceremonies for relating to deities and ancestors; and a reservoir of Power accessible through magic for dealing with such day-to-day problems as illness, assault by enemies, and difficult decision-making. Now the important question: How well could African captives carry its religion across the Atlantic? Some writers contend that amid the horrors of capture, passage, and the slave regime Africans could not preserve much of their traditional religion, so that after two or three generations it was obliterated. At the opposite extreme are those who suggest that black religion in the United States consists mostly of African features thinly overlaid with Euro-American Christianity. This debate about "African survivals" is important today. Many blacks do not like to think that their ancestors were emptied of their authentic heritage, leaving a vacuum that was filled with the religion of white oppressors. In any case most scholars now agree that the truth in the debate over African survivals is found somewhere between the two extreme positions stated above. On the one hand, it is clear that the religion of most blacks in America today is within the Christian tradition. On the other hand, it is no longer possible to deny that aspects of the religion of Africa have been transmitted through the generations in this country, though not as visibly as among blacks in South America and the Caribbean. It is now known that slaves struggled with much success to maintain stable families, which allowed them to transmit their own beliefs and values. It must also be remembered that Africans were imported in large numbers up to 1808 and in smaller numbers up to the Civil War. Thus a high percentage of American blacks had contacts with native Africans all during the slave period, through whom they could renew their awareness and appreciation of African ways. Finally, religious beliefs and practices, valued in the struggle for survival in a hostile environment, were also relatively easy to disguise or conceal from unfriendly eyes. As a result, American black religion emerged as a blend of early American Christianity and African traditional religion. People were not conscious of the blending. Whatever they encountered in this country they shaped through their unique perspective as Africans rather than Europeans and as slaves in a nation where freedom was a special point of pride. The result was different from the religion of Africa and from white Christianity.

The Black Encounter With White Protestantism

As tens of thousands of Africans arrived in the British colonies, very few church people worried about the religious status of the black slaves. Even though Christians were supposed to be eager to convert non-Christians, there were powerful reasons why whites in the eighteenth century did not make great efforts to convert blacks.

In the first place, most of the Christians involved were Protestants, who were about two hundred years behind the Catholics in developing missions to foreign lands and to non-Christians in their colonies. During the eighteenth century, when most of the African captives arrived in North America, only a few ministers tried to convert blacks or to persuade others to do so. These people produced a lot of speeches and pamphlets but relatively little action. This is explained partly by the shortage of ministers and other persons qualified to instruct slaves. Unlike Catholics, Protestants had no religious orders; nearly all ministers were attached to parishes or congregations. Teaching slaves would therefore be an extra duty and would depend entirely upon the zeal of the minister and the attitude of his congregation.

This leads us to other reasons why blacks were not widely exposed to Christian instruction in the eighteenth century. Some whites believed that Africans had no souls, that they were "creatures of another species, who had no right to be instructed or admitted to the sacraments." At the same time, some slave owners feared that slaves who were baptized into the Christian faith would be legally entitled to their freedom. It is not clear where they got this idea. No colonial judge had ever freed a slave on account of baptism, and in earlier centuries European Christians had regularly owned Christian slaves. Nevertheless, ministers intent on "christianizing" the slaves worked hard to convince owners that Christian slaves were still slaves. Some colonial legislatures passed laws stating the same thing, and gradually the idea died out.

Another objection to converting slaves was the fear that sharing the masters' religion would make them harder to control, encouraging them even to run away or to attack their owners. It is true that Christianity did inspire some later slave rebellions, but the evidence is unclear for the eighteenth century. In any case, church leaders who wanted to convert slaves had to convince whites that Christianity would make slaves easier to control, not harder.

The result of all this was that few slaves had the chance to receive instruction or to convert to Christianity. Those who had the chance often had reasons for refusing to convert. They were not permitted to "add" Jesus Christ to the deities of Africa. Rather they were supposed to give up the old ways altogether, which they were often unwilling to do. Also the version of Christianity offered to them was one that emphasized obeying their masters and mistresses, and that was not the message they wanted to hear. Some of them resisted Christianity simply because it was the religion of the oppressors. If they did convert and become church members, the whites did not treat them as spiritual equals. They had to sit in some remote part of the church, and they could not receive Holy Communion until all the whites were finished. Under these conditions, not many blacks chose to become Christians. Even the revivalism of the Great Awakening, and its southern aftermath, was directed mainly to whites and made only a slight impression on the black population. Before 1800 it is estimated that no more than one black person in fifty was baptized. An even smaller number became church members.

In the 1780s and 1790s, there were signs that the situation was changing. More blacks were attracted to Christianity, and more whites were willing to encourage black conversions. After 1800, these trends were accelerated until an Afro-American version of Christianity was widespread among the black population. Although our understanding of this change is far from complete, it is possible to suggest some of the reasons for it.

From the white side, probably the most important reason was the increase in the number of white church members. Traveling ministers and camp meetings spread the revivalist version of Protestantism to the westward-moving whites. Many older churches in the East, and particularly the Southeast, were also swept by the revival spirit. Consequently, a larger portion of the white population became religiously committed and began to worry about the salvation of the blacks. They believed not only that they had a religious duty to convert slaves but also that converted slaves would be more loyal and obedient to their masters. Therefore more owners began to permit ministers to preach to their slaves, as long as the ministers agreed — and many did — that slavery was agreeable to God and beneficial to blacks. It was helpful, too, that the revivalist emphasis on an inward experience of conversion did not require teaching slaves to read religious literature, as earlier methods of slave conversion had required. After 1800, and even more after 1831, most owners and southern lawmakers agreed that slaves should be kept illiterate as a safety measure. Increasingly, then, in the period from 1800 to the Civil War, slaves were exposed to efforts to convert them to Christianity.

There were also developments from the black side that led to greater interest in Christianity. For one thing, the percentage of African-born blacks was diminishing in comparison to the number of their American-born descendants. The latter group, having better knowledge of American language and customs, were in a better position to adopt and modify whatever features of white society were relevant to their needs. Sometimes that included the Christian religion. Another development was the emancipation of slaves in the North during and after the Revolution. As a result, the number of free blacks grew to about 10 percent of the black population. Free blacks were strongly attracted to Christianity and very energetic in struggling to establish congregations and denominations independent of white control.

Most important of all, blacks became increasingly skillful at interpreting the Christian religion in ways that were relevant to slave existence and racial oppression. Specifically, they saw God and Jesus as supporting them in their tribulation; they saw Christian "freedom" as meaning liberation from slavery; and they saw slaveholders as sinners. These ideas, together with surviving elements of African religion, formed the basis for a distinctive version of Christianity that angered and frightened most whites whenever they became aware of it. Most of the time blacks were careful to hide the true nature of their religious beliefs. There is no doubt that this version of Christianity owed something to the handful of white ministers who insisted that the God of Jesus Christ was opposed to slavery. But it was spread most effectively by the growing corps of black clergy, both slave and free. We will look first at slave religion and then at the churches of the free blacks.

Slave Religion

The religion of southern slaves flourished in a variety of settings. There were some formally constituted black churches, mostly in towns and mostly Baptist. The founding of the earliest one is usually dated around 1775, but one scholar believes that an earlier church existed in 1758 (Sobel, 296). Such congregations existed under different degrees of white supervision and harassment. Following slave conspiracies and rebellions, such as those in 1800 and 1822 and 1831, whites reacted by further restricting or even closing black churches in the area. Nevertheless, several such congregations existed at the time of emancipation. In several towns, slaves were members of mixed churches controled by the white membership.

On farms and plantations, there were sometimes informally organized black congregations, supervised but operating openly. Some plantations had chapels, where slaves worshiped with the families of the owner and the overseer. Finally, clusters of slaves risked severe punishment by meeting secretly to share words and worship practices not approved by white ministers and masters. This underground slave movement is referred to as the secret church or "the invisible institution." These various settings — organized or informal, mixed or all-black, public or secret — were interrelated. Slaves might hear a visiting white preacher on Sunday afternoon and then gather secretly in a swamp or thicket the next night to pray and hear a black preacher.

Conversion. The majority of religious slaves shared the main features of the revivalist viewpoint described in the preceding chapter. For them, the gateway to salvation was an identifiable experience of conversion, which took place in two stages. First, God "convicted" a person of sin. This was experienced as "heaviness of soul" and fear of hell, leading the sinner toward sincere repentance. Then came the second stage: pardon and rescue by God through Christ. This was felt as "saving faith" and the assurance of forgiveness and acceptance before God. The burden was lifted from the soul, and joy flooded in. Ordinarily, the whole episode took place in the realm of thought and feeling; no vision or trance was required. Yet a certain number of slaves reported visions that reveal the intensity and meaning of conversion. Images of Satan and hell would sometimes enliven the conviction stage, after which the penitent might see New Jerusalem shining in the heavens, with God on his throne declaring the sinner's forgiveness.

And then came the joy: "I ran to an elm tree and tried to put my arms around it. Never had I felt such love before. It just looked like I loved everything and everybody" (Raboteau, 270).

Spirituals. Slaves created forms of worship that expressed the unique situation of captives in the land of the free. In particular, they created the black spirituals, religious songs of deep insight and rare beauty. The spirituals were made out of many elements: Bible texts, phrases from sermons, African tunes and rhythms, camp meeting hymns, and ballads. These elements were combined and shaped in the potent atmosphere of slave worship. "The way we worshiped is almost indescribable," wrote slave preacher James L. Smith. "The singing was accompanied by a certain ecstasy of motion, clapping of hands, tossing of heads, which would continue without cessation about half an hour; one would lead off in a kind of recitative style, others joining in the chorus" (Raboteau, 243-244). Some spirituals were used to accompany the worship act called the "ring shout," a religious circle-dance popular among blacks in some areas of the South.

Spirituals provided one of the best sources for understanding the religious beliefs of the slaves. For instance, they spoke of the tribulation of slave life ("I'm bowed down with a burden of woe"), often connecting their own suffering with the suffering of Jesus ("Oh, dey whupped him up de hill"). Each one walked "that lonesome road" with Death waiting, Death aided by the rigors of the slave regime ("Death ain't nothin' but a robber, don't you see"). But the robber did not have the last word: "An' de Lord shall bear my spirit home."

It would be a mistake to suppose that references to a happy afterlife meant that slaves were resigned to the injustices of this life. They condemned the slaveholders not only by singing about suffering but also by singing of freedom. In some songs they were the enslaved Children of Israel awaiting liberation:

> *Go down, Moses, 'way down in Egypt land;*
> *Tell ol' Pharoah,*
> *Let my people go.*
>
> . . . .
>
> *My Lord delivered Daniel,*
> *Why can't he deliver me?*

When emancipation came, "blacks viewed it as an act of God analogous to Israel's exodus from Egypt" (Cone, 1972, 45).

Slavery chain broke down at last, broke at last,
broke at last,
Slavery chain done broke at last,
Goin' to praise God till I die.

Preaching. Slaves accepted and reaffirmed the Protestant emphasis on the preaching of sermons as an indispensable act of worship. Sermons were used to instruct, reprove, convert, and unify the people. To perform these tasks, black preachers developed special forms of oratory. As with the spirituals, black preaching was made up of elements drawn from different sources, but the result was a distinctive product of the slave community.

Two features of the black preaching style should be noted. One is the "moaning" or chanting mode of delivery. A preacher would phrase the first part of his address in ordinary tones and cadences. But sometimes as the sermon progressed his delivery would shift to the moaning style, half spoken and half sung. It was a powerful mode of presentation. He could tell a story in that way; he could urge a response; or he could evoke a mood of sorrow or jubilation. Another noteworthy feature of early black preaching was "call and response." The preacher did not intend to deliver a monologue but to enter into a kind of dialogue with the people, spontaneous yet ritualized. The customs of slave worship were such that a preacher would have felt frustrated and isolated in the absence of audible responses from the people. Some white congregations responded audibly, too, but black responses were generally more complex, more persistent, and more intense. Black people would respond by echoing the preacher's phrases or by shouting encouragement ("Tell it," "Hit him again") or by expressing their moods ("Glory," "Mercy"). Sometimes the responses included clapping, weeping, lifting arms toward heaven, or "doing a little shout" (dance), as God's Spirit dictated.

Who were these slave preachers? They were men who felt called by God to speak to the people. But it was up to the people to confirm that a man had the power to preach. He was a man, therefore, who was respected by others. Although there were privileges attached to his office, such as having permission to travel in the neighborhood and being excused from field work, there were also problems and dangers. Whites counted on black preachers to keep slaves pacified and were suspicious of preachers who seemed too popular. So when whites were present, preachers had to urge slaves to be obedient and loyal. Punishment was swift and severe for those who refused. On the other hand, most preachers were convinced that the true Christian message was connected with freedom from slavery, and they said so whenever they could. Anderson Edwards, looking back on his years as a slave preacher in Texas, explained that he could give his people the true message only "on the sly," but that he often took the opportunity to tell them in secret that God was going to set them free (Levine, 48).

Religion and Resistance. One question that arises often about slave religion is whether it tended to make slaves accept their slavery or instead to make them resist it. It has been said that slave religion emphasized emotional ecstasies and promises of heaven after death, and that such "otherworldly" themes lulled slaves into accepting their status rather than struggling against it. On the other hand, we can argue that "acceptance" and "resistance" are false alternatives. The real question for slaves was how best to promote their interests under an oppressive system that they could not destroy. "Resistance" was any action that increased their well-being, that injured owners or their property, or that slowed the system down. Slaves engaged in countless such actions, usually in the belief that their religion supported and even required that form of behavior.

The most spectacular kinds of resistance were assassination and armed rebellion. The three best-known plans for rebellions were those of Gabriel Prosser in 1800, Denmark Vesey in 1822, and Nat Turner in 1831. Each one of these men was a respected religious leader. Each one was convinced that God supported the insurrection, and their followers agreed. Another way to resist was to escape to the northern states or Canada. Another was sabotage: burning buildings, breaking equipment, injuring or killing livestock. Or one could pretend to be sick or injured. One could even injure oneself, to deprive the master of labor. Then there was stealing from slaveholders to improve one's diet. In general, black religion supported these actions. There were disagreements, of course, and some hard ethical decisions. But the understanding was that God hated slavery and true Christians should fight it in any way they could.

From this angle, the matter of "otherworldliness" takes on a new appearance. Slaves refused to be limited by the possibilities of this world, where slaveholders prospered and blacks were bought and sold like cattle. Religious slaves had no doubt that those who died in bondage would be taken "home" to heaven. The effect of that belief was to keep people from despair and madness, not to make them accept slavery as God's will for black people. If slaveholders continued holding out against God's will, then God would deliver his oppressed people in "a truer world," where justice prevailed. Such faith nerved all sorts of heroic resistance, as well as supporting the dreary and hazardous day-to-day lives of the majority of slaves.

Northern Churches

Although Africans were imported for lifetime servitude, there were some blacks who were not slaves. Individual owners liberated slaves for various reasons. A few slaves were allowed to earn money and eventually buy their freedom. Sympathetic whites sometimes bought slaves in order to free them. Freed blacks worked to buy their families out of slavery. Some men were freed in exchange for military service in the War of Independence. And then, between 1777 and 1804, courts and legislatures freed most of the slaves in the northern states. By 1820, about one-tenth of the black people were legally free. (Some free blacks lived in the South, but as time went on it became harder for them to avoid re-enslavement.)

To be free, however, did not mean having the privileges of white citizens. Cities and states enacted laws restricting the activities of free blacks. Unwritten custom hampered them still further. Black children could rarely attend white schools. Hospitals were segregated. By 1840, less than 7 percent of northern blacks were legally entitled to vote. An 1821 description of the plight of Pennsylvania's free blacks applied to other states as well: they were "excluded from most of the respectable and profitable employments of life, confined to the humblest and least gainful occupations, with strong prejudices to surmount, and labouring under every species of difficulty" (Scherer, 120-121).

These conditions affected church life, too. After the Revolution the number of black church members increased. They were barred from official positions, except for serving other black members. They were seated separately or obliged to attend worship and instruction at different times from the whites. So even in the supposed solidarity of Christian fellowship, blacks felt the pain of racial subordination. In this atmosphere, the northern black churches were created by the separation of the black and white members of mixed churches. Although whites were generally happy to get rid of the blacks, it was usually the blacks who initiated the separation by formally requesting to be "honorably dismissed" to form a new congregation. Sometimes the separation went smoothly, but on other occasions, the whites made trouble by trying to retain control over the religious affairs of the black group.

The best-known of these cases involved Richard Allen, a leader of the Black members of the St. George Methodist Church in Philadelphia. Even though the blacks were regarded as a nuisance, they were not allowed to form a self-governing congregation. Matters came to a climax in a humiliating episode in 1787. Allen, Absalom Jones, and other blacks were apparently uncertain about where they were expected to sit after the church had been remodeled. They took the "wrong" seats, with the result that a white trustee pulled Jones to his feet during prayer in an effort to make him change places. The whole black group walked out in protest and soon formed the Free African Society, which functioned for a time as a church. Then, in 1794, most of the group formed an Episcopalian congregation with Jones as pastor. Allen, however, organized a Methodist congregation. White Methodists ultimately refused to cooperate in this venture, excommunicating Allen and some others instead of honorably dismissing them. In 1816, the Philadelphia group joined with black Methodists elsewhere to form the first independent black denomination, the African Methodist Episcopal Church. Allen was the first bishop. Other black congregations joined together as the African Methodist Episcopal Zion Church in 1820.

Meanwhile, independent black Baptist congregations appeared in northern cities (as distinguished from earlier Baptist churches in the South, most of whose members were slaves). Three churches were established in 1809: the first African Baptist Church in Philadelphia was formed by black members of a mixed church; the African Baptist Church in Joy Street, Boston, was formed under the leadership of Thomas Paul; and the Abyssinian Baptist Church in New York was constituted, with the same Thomas Paul as sponsor. Black Presbyterians, Episcopalians, and Congregationalists also formed a handful of churches, but Methodists and Baptists predominated.

As indicated, white northerners were often hostile to black religious independence. Black ministers traveling to serve and organize blacks in newly settled areas could not count on hospitality or even safety except among their own people and with a few sympathetic whites. But despite the risks, the black churches did expand and consolidate without white supervision in a way that was not permitted in the South before emancipation. Black Baptist progress westward was marked by the development of associations of congregations for mutual support and counsel. In 1836, Ohio Baptists founded the Providence Baptist Association, the first black Baptist organization larger than a single congregation. Two years later, the Wood River Association was organized by black Baptists in Illinois. In 1844, the African Methodist Episcopal Church, largest of the black Methodist groups, reported forty-seven congregations west of the Alleghenies.

Among the distinctive features of the northern black churches was a concern over slavery as a religious issue. Though free, they could not easily forget the slaves. Many northerners had been slaves and were either legally free or fugitives from the slave states. Many had loved ones still in bondage. The issue was brought home in a new way after 1850, when the new federal Fugitive Slave Act forced many ministers and church members to flee to Canada. It is not surprising, therefore, to find that blacks were heavily involved in the abolition movement. They, more than whites and at greater risk, assisted slaves to escape. Very few whites shared the eagerness to abolish slavery that was a normal part of black consciousness. And very few white Christians believed, as black Christians did, that God hated slavery and wanted his people to fight it by every available means.

After Emancipation

The Emancipation Proclamation took effect on January 1, 1863, and slavery was legally abolished almost three years later with the ratification of the Thirteenth Amendment. Although there was general rejoicing over abolition, blacks understood that they would have to take vigorous steps to achieve a tolerable place in American society. Although they put forth great effort, ending in martyrdom for some, they reckoned without the power and determination of whites to devise alternative ways to keep blacks in subjection.

Land ownership and education were the most urgent goals of ex-slaves, while civil rights and political participation were the main concerns of teachers and ministers and other black leaders. All of these goals were pursued and in some degree achieved during the period of Reconstruction. But within a decade after the Civil War, white politics shifted, leaving blacks with little power and few white allies. The great majority of whites in all regions believed that the former Confederate states should manage "their" black people in any way they saw fit. After

1877, blacks were deprived of the vote by law, fraud, and violence. Land ownership, never far advanced among exslaves, was discouraged by the same means. Sharecropping became the destiny of most blacks, and in many cases that system amounted to peonage. Educational opportunities were restricted by means that included burning schoolhouses and murdering teachers. By the end of the century, a rash of new segregation laws condemned blacks to inferior public services and facilities, or excluded them altogether.

Against this background of shattered dreams, the black churches entered a period of unparalleled growth. The black scholar and leader W.E.B. DuBois estimated that on the eve of the Civil War about 11 percent of American blacks were church members, while by 1903 (when he was writing) the figure had grown to 33 percent. DuBois claimed that "in the South, at least, practically every American Negro is a church member." Allowing for some exaggeration, it is clear that blacks embraced their churches at an astonishing rate, as if catching up after the restrictions of slave days.

The reasons for this huge institutional growth are not hard to find. Most blacks regarded white influence in religion as a corruption of true faith, if for no other reason than that whites had generally supported slavery. Given the opportunity, blacks removed themselves from this bad influence. This process sometimes resembled the earlier separations in the North. Among Baptists, the process was relatively easy, because the decisions were entirely local. If black and white members agreed that separation was a good thing, then nothing more was required. The matter was more complicated for Methodists, because ministers were appointed by bishops and property was held in trust by regional "conferences." However, the main body of southern white Methodists agreed to permit its black members to form a separate denomination, which was constituted in 1870 as the Colored (now Christian) Methodist Episcopal Church. Smaller denominations achieved similar results.

This relatively simple picture was complicated by the fact that northern organizations, black and white, sent missionaries into the South. The aim of many of these workers was primarily educational, and their legacy consisted of schools and colleges for young blacks. But in other cases the purpose was to convert and organize church members. Ministers of the African Methodist Episcopal and African Methodist Episcopal Zion churches, who had been barred from the South before emancipation, now made up for lost time. They found thousands of people eager to affiliate with churches that had been free of white control for many years. Northern black Baptists also organized themselves for work in the South and were responsible for founding or reconstituting many churches, especially in the Mississippi Valley and farther west where many exslaves had migrated. In the South, many associations were formed, as well as state organizations called "conventions." This development culminated in the creation of a nationwide black Baptist body in 1895, the National Baptist Convention.

Up to this point, it has been appropriate to view the growth of black churches in terms of Baptists and Methodists. Other black Protestants together with black Catholics made up a small percentage of black church members. However, just before the First World War, a new religious movement arose, called Pentecostalism. It made a significant impression on the white population, but an even greater one on the blacks, growing into the third largest black religious affiliation.

Pentecostal groups have the same general features as other churches of the Protestant revivalist tradition, both black and white, requiring a definite experience of conversion through saving faith in Christ. But Pentecostal groups, which blacks often refer to as Sanctified churches, have additional marks to distinguish them from others. One is a generally stricter standard of Christian behavior — "living holy" as some blacks say — including avoiding personal adornment and worldly amusements. But more important as a distinguishing mark is their belief in the Baptism of the Holy Ghost, defined as another definite experience from God subsequent to conversion. The sign of this "work of grace" is that a person begins "speaking in tongues," that is, uttering ecstatic sounds without conscious effort or control. Pentecostals at times debate whether these syllables are modern foreign languages or "unknown tongues," perhaps of ancient peoples or angels. Pentecostals also emphasize other "gifts of the Spirit," such as healing of diseases.

Certain features of slave religion and of other nineteenth-century religious movements may be viewed as forerunners of Pentecostalism. But all of these tendencies came together in a revival in the warehouse district in Los Angeles. All of the Pentecostal churches today, both black and white, can be traced back to an extended revival, from 1906 to 1909, three years of daily meetings led by William J. Seymour, a black minister in his fifties with both Methodist and Baptist affiliations in his background. The location was an abandoned church-turned-stable on Azusa Street. The furniture consisted of planks and barrels and crates. Seymour urged people to pray specifically for the Baptism of the Holy Spirit. Some people were struck with the "gift of tongues" the moment they entered the building; others struggled many days for the same blessing. The Azusa Street revival was publicized internationally in the press and by word of mouth. Reporters expressed admiration or ridicule, approval or alarm. People traveled from across the nation and from other countries, returning home to tell others.

Although the Azusa Street revival was interracial, the Pentecostal movement that flowed from it quickly divided into white and black streams. At the conclusion of the daily meetings in 1909, whites withdrew from Azusa Street Mission to form their own church. In other parts of the country, whites and blacks formed dozens of racially separate organizations. Seymour, though he traveled sometimes as a visiting evangelist, did not expand his authority beyond the Azusa Street Mission, which did not survive long after his death around 1920. Of the black Sanctified groups that sprang from his work, probably the largest is the Church of God in Christ, consisting of more than four thousand congregations.

Black Religion In The Cities

After the Civil War, blacks began moving slowly northward, westward, and cityward. These movements were greatly speeded up around the time of the First World War. Good pay in expanding industries was the main attraction, while in the South repeated crop failures and deteriorating race relations encouraged people to leave. In 1910, three-quarters of American blacks lived in rural areas and 90 percent lived in the former slave states. By 1965, three-quarters lived in cities and half of the black population was outside the former slave states. The shift brought grave new problems, as well as new opportunities. Urban whites reacted decisively to contain the new black population in separate residential areas. The jobs available were mainly those that could not be filled by white workers. School systems allocated fewer resources to areas where black children lived. The situation was greatly worsened by the Great Depression of the 1930s and somewhat improved by the prosperity following the Second World War.

For church people, too, the Great Migration to the cities brought new opportunities and new worries. Religious life, it seemed, did not hold together in the city as it did in the country. The Klan might terrorize the southern countryside, but Satan apparently reigned over the northern city streets. Religious people were quick to observe the theaters, the dance halls, and the bars where you could hear the devil's own music, the blues. In the country, the black church was the main center not only for religious expression and solemn reflection on life and death, but also for self-improvement, group action, and entertainment. Even people who were not deeply religious were drawn to the church for a variety of reasons. The city, however, offered alternative ways of fulfilling personal and social needs, so many people drifted away from the churches. Although black church people managed to bring a large number of each new generation into the churches, there were highly visible alternatives in the ghetto, where a sensitive youngster could see religion not only neglected but ridiculed.

New residents in the cities discovered another problem. They found carefully preserved class distinctions within the black communities, sharper than the ones they had known in the country, and these distinctions affected religion along with everything else. Sociologists would identify a small but highly visible upper class, mostly well-educated professionals. In a somewhat larger middle class were government and clerical employees and skilled workers, as well as most of the business people (all but the most successful). The mass of blacks belonged to the lower class, consisting of unskilled laborers, domestic and other "service" workers, and people on welfare.

Upper class blacks tended to prefer the predominantly white denominations, such as the Presbyterian, Episcopalian, or Congregationalist, though they often belonged to all-black congregations of these denominations. Such a church drew its minister from the ranks of college and seminary graduates, hoping to be community leaders in social reform (like the Social Gospel ministers in Chapter Three), and expected to deliver well-prepared, informative, and uplifting sermons.

The upper class also accounted for most of the few black Catholics in the United States. Throughout the nineteenth century, the Catholic Church had been overwhelmed with the problems of white immigrants and had little energy for missions to blacks. Except in New Orleans and some smaller places, few blacks were exposed to Catholicism. Besides, most blacks shared the anti-Catholic sentiments of white Protestants, while the flood of new white Catholics — often competing with blacks for employment — quickly acquired the racial prejudice of native-born Americans. The first black priest to serve in the

United States was not ordained until 1888. Nevertheless, in some cities there were black Catholic parishes, often operating fine schools, drawn largely from the upper class. In the 1950s, when some white Catholics took courageous stands on behalf of black rights, Catholicism began appealing to a larger number of blacks from a wider band of the social spectrum.

Blacks in the middle class preferred the larger African Methodist denominations and, in second place, certain Baptist churches. Middle class churches displayed features of quiet worship combined with parts of the livelier worship pattern of the rural South. In such a church, the minister, a man of some educational attainment, perhaps a college graduate, had to be sensitive to the dual expectations of his people. His sermons were expected to be clear and well-organized, but with some traditional tales and some tones and cadences in the old-time style.

However, it was the churches of the black majority that made the most creative innovations and displayed the greatest variety of expression, while seeking to preserve the style and values of country religion. Some of these churches were Methodist, a much larger group were Baptist, and a growing number were Sanctified, fanning out from Azusa Street. One of the features of the lower class churches was that so many of them were housed in rented stores and private residences. In most cases, the poverty of the members dictated such facilities. But people spoke positively of the intimacy of these small churches in contrast to the much larger churches housed in great brick or stone buildings. Indeed, it was possible in these storefront churches to duplicate the close social ties of the rural South. Sometimes these small congregations were like extended families, providing emotional support and other forms of mutual aid.

The minister of such a church was not expected to have much formal education, seldom as much as a high school diploma before the Second World War. But he was expected to show signs that he was "called by God" to assume the ministerial office. The foremost sign was the ability to deliver stirring sermons in the vigorous manner of the old folk preacher, including the moaning style. If in addition he showed talents for keeping peace among his people, and for helping them solve day-to-day problems, then he could count on a grateful following.

It was in these churches of the black majority, especially the Sanctified ones, that a new type of religious music arose, called the gospel song. At a time when spirituals had lost their power in the urban churches and church music was in a state of confusion, gospel singing "helped bring back into black church music the sounds and the structure of the folk spirituals [and] work songs" (Levine, 185). That old stream of Afro-American music had been taken up in "the devil's music" — blues, ragtime, and jazz — so carefully avoided by church people. But then in the teens and twenties of this century some black Christians, beginning with the Sanctified groups, came to believe that "the devil should not be allowed to keep all this good rhythm" (Levine, 180). So the bluesy, jazzy sounds returned to the church in the form of gospel singing, made famous by Mahalia Jackson and a host of other musicians. From the 1930s to the present, gospel songs have displaced the spirituals as the main form of black religious music.

Religion and Freedom

Following the Second World War, the black churches prospered along with other religious groups from the surge of religious interest and affiliation. Then, in the late fifties, they gained added strength from the Black Freedom Movement. Encouraged by the school desegregation decision of 1954 and the Civil Rights Act of 1957, the Movement began with the lunch counter sit-ins and the Montgomery bus boycott. The goals of the Movement were the registration of black voters and the integration of public accommodations, schools, and transportation. The most prominent leader was a young Baptist minister named Martin Luther King, Jr., whose inspiring addresses were in the tradition of the black pulpit. Southern churches became rallying points for marches and other protest activities. King believed that black protest and suffering would produce not only freedom for blacks, but also reconciliation with whites. The presence of many whites among the protesters in the streets, in southern jails, and among the Movement's martyrs seemed to confirm King's view.

But then the Movement faltered. Even before King's assassination in 1968, some young blacks began to question his strategy and tactics. In 1966, Stokely Carmichael coined the slogan "Black Power," which implied a rejection of King's point about reconciliation, replacing it with an emphasis upon black autonomy: blacks applying pressure however and wherever they could, in order to secure their own liberation. Black Power leaders spoke against the black churches, saying that Christianity was the oppressor's religion. Black Christians were unreliable revolutionaries; they were Uncle Toms brainwashed by white religion into accepting second-class status. Particularly in the North, many blacks voiced disrespect for the churches. Non-Christian religions flourished, especially Islam. An American-oriented group, the Nation of Islam, sometimes called the Black Muslims, grew under the leadership of Elijah Muhammad and is now led by his son Wallace Muhammad.

At the same time, there were a number of black Christian leaders who were sympathetic with the aims and mood of Black Power. They set out to show that, while white Christianity was false because it supported slavery and racism, black Christianity and black liberation were truly partners. The most prominent and productive writer among these people has been James H. Cone, who in a series of books and articles beginning in 1968 has analyzed Christian theology in the light of the black struggle. Cone's theological position is that Christ is the divine Liberator. God's will is the liberation of the oppressed. Although liberation will ultimately produce reconciliation, the immediate effect will be to destroy the power and wealth of the oppressors. True Christians struggle vigorously for liberation with all available means, thus obeying God's will.

It is clear that the black religious experience cannot be stereotyped or captured in a brief description. Indeed, variety and flexibility have been necessities for survival from the secret church to the storefront. At the same time, there is a distinctiveness and stability in black religion that testifies to a history of heartbreaking struggle and to hidden sources of strength.

Selected People and Events

1441 A Portuguese ship carried a cargo of gold and slaves from Africa to Lisbon; beginning of the Atlantic slave trade.

1619 A Dutch warship landed a small group of Africans in Jamestown, Virginia; first blacks in the future United States of America.

1661 First statute in North America referring to slavery, but evidence shows that blacks had been customarily enslaved for many years in the British colonies.

1701 Founding of the Society for the Propagation of the Gospel in Foreign Parts (SPG), a British society encompassing, among other aims, the first organized effort to convert North American slaves.

1758 Reported existence of a Baptist congregation at Silver Bluff, South Carolina; often identified as the first black church in North America.

1787 Richard Allen (1760-1831) and others left a Philadelphia church service in protest over treatment of black members; event led to the formation of the African Methodist Episcopal Church in 1816.

1836 Formation of the Providence Baptist Association in Ohio, the first organization of black Baptists congregations.

1843 Henry Highland Grant (1815-1881), a black Presbyterian minister, delivered his "Address to the Slaves of the United States of America," urging slaves to rebel in God's name.

1865 Slavery was abolished by the ratification of the Thirteenth Amendment.

1866 Henry McNeal Turner (1831-1915) was appointed to organize the expansion of the African Methodist Episcopal Church in Georgia; example of rapid growth of black churches in the South after emancipation. Later a bishop, Turner became an advocate of black emigration to Africa.

1888 Augustus Tolan, born a slave in Missouri, was ordained, becoming the birst black Roman Catholic priest to serve in the United States.

1890 The Mississippi Legislature amended the state constitution to deprive blacks of the vote; other southern states soon followed.

1895 Baptists gathered in Atlanta, Georgia, and formed the National Baptist Convention, the first black Baptist denomination, with Elias Camp Morris as first president.

1903 W.E. Burghardt (1868-1963), black sociologist, historian, and protest leader, published *The Negro Church,* the first sociological study of black religion.

1906 Beginning of the Azusa Street revival in Los Angeles, California; founding event of modern Pentecostalism; led by the black minister William J. Seymour (1855?-1920?).

1918 End of the First World War led to numerous lynchings and other assaults on blacks; contributed to the Great Migration to northern cities.

1930 Thomas A. Dorsey (1899-), pioneer composer of gospel songs, performed "If You See My Savior" for the National Baptist Convention, leading to a major breakthrough in the acceptability and popularity of gospel songs in the churches.

1955 Beginning of the Montgomery, Alabama, bus boycott, which raised Martin Luther King, Jr. (1929-1968), to national prominence as a leader of the black protest movement.

1966 Publication of a statement by a large committee of prominent black church leaders endorsing the protest movement and using the expression "Black Power."

CHAPTER FIVE

Catholicism: Tradition and Change

As with Protestants, the main determinant of Catholic strength in this country has been the pattern of immigration from Europe. Catholics did not begin arriving here in large numbers until after 1830, over a half-century after independence. This meant that Protestants had more than two centuries of unchallenged religious monopoly in this land before the great Catholic migrations. But once Catholics began coming, pushed by adverse conditions in Europe and pulled by promises of a secure future in the United States, they arrived in astonishing numbers. The percentage of Catholics in the American population grew enormously, as these figures show:

1790	1 percent
1850	7
1900	15
1925	25

Since 1925, when new laws reduced Catholic immigration to a near standstill, the figure has remained constant. For over a century, the Roman Catholic Church has been the largest single religious organization in the United States. It is larger than even the most numerous Protestant "families": Lutheran, Baptist, or Methodist.

Spanish and French Beginnings

Catholicism in the New World began with the colonizing ventures of Spain. Starting with a settlement on the island of Hispaniola founded during the second voyage of Christopher Columbus in 1493, Catholicism was introduced over a century before French and Spanish colonization. During the sixteenth century, Spaniards conquered an American empire stretching from the tip of South America northward through Mexico and the Caribbean. The northernmost reaches of that empire were Florida on the east and California on the west. Forty-two years before the English established Protestantism on this continent, San Augustin (St. Augustine, Florida), the first Roman Catholic parish within the eventual boundaries of the United States, was founded in 1565.

The northernmost regions of the Spanish Empire are often referred to as the "borderlands." Removed from the center of Spanish American power and culture, the borderlands figured in imperial strategy as a protection against encroachment by other powers. A few thousand soldiers, priests, traders, and their families were outnumbered by native Americans. Religious and political institutions were trimmed to the basics.

The most important religious institutions were the Indian missions conducted by several religious orders, most prominently the Jesuits and the Franciscans. At their peak in the late nineteenth century, the missions numbered a hundred or so, extending from San Augustin in Florida to San Francisco in California. Each had a church in the center of a large tract of land. The idea was to make each mission into a community of converted Indians, who would become farmers under the direction of the priests. These missions displayed the usual ambiguities of colonial missionary enterprises. Often courageous and compassionate in carrying out their work, the missionaries were intensely dedicated to securing the eternal salvation of their Indian clients. At the same time, they were agents of the Empire, convinced that salvation required the converts to submit to the Crown and to change their lives to conform with Spanish patterns. Although the missionaries resisted efforts to enslave Indians, their own system often amounted to a form of peonage.

Spanish dominion in the New World dissolved in the nineteenth century, as revolutions produced independent nations, such as Mexico in 1821. Between 1819 and 1854, the United States secured by purchase, conquest, and annexation those portions of the former Spanish Empire that are now Florida and the southwestern United States. The Catholic hierarchy of the United States assumed responsibility for the remnants of over two centuries of missionary effort. Since then, immigration from Mexico and other southern lands has guaranteed that the Spanish heritage will continue as an important element of Catholicism in the United States.

The French followed the Spanish, becoming the second great Catholic power to colonize the continent. Controlling portions of North America from 1604 to 1763, the French occupied points form Acadia (later Nova Scotia) to the center of the continent and from Hudson's Bay to the mouth of the Mississippi. Missionaries, especially Jesuit priests, led the way in exploring these regions and creating French settlements. The best known of these was Jacques Marquette (1637-1675), who with the trader Louis Joliet traveled by canoe from northern Lake Michigan to the lower Mississippi River. In addition to Jesuits, other orders of priests established missions and schools. Nuns and laywomen were active in the religious leadership of New France and Louisiana, especially in founding schools and hospitals.

Like the Spanish, the French emphasized and utilized the Indian mission. French priests showed great concern for the souls of the Indians, and many priests were killed in the line of duty. In some cases, there was a genuine interest in Indian culture. But French priests also served imperial interests by persuading their Indian clients to fight against the British, who also had Indian allies. As a result, Indian wars were inspired by Europeans. For instance, the British supported the Iroquois in their successful war with the Hurons, who were allied with the French. The war for dominion between France and Britain also had another religious connection. It was a contest between Catholic power and Protestant power, between "papists" and "heretics." The pattern of religious bitterness was magnified by this warfare and was carried forward into the religious history of the United States.

Britain drove the French from power in North America in 1763. But French culture survived in eastern

Canada and more tenuously around New Orleans. Scores of French place names in the United States mark the former extent of New France and French Louisiana. Only a few thousand families in the country maintain the language and heritage of those early French colonists. However, in the nineteenth century, a significant immigration of French priests and nuns assisted in the development of the Catholic Church in the new United States.

British North America and The Early United States

Despite the priority of Spanish and French Catholics on this continent, the continuous history of the Catholic Church in the United States begins with the handful of British and Irish Catholics who migrated to the British colonies in the seventeenth and eighteenth centuries. Long years of warfare between Protestant and Catholic countries guaranteed that neither would have much toleration for members of the opposing faith. The French and Spanish were harshly intolerant of Protestants both in Europe and America. The British cruelly opposed Catholics in Britain and Ireland and — somewhat less vigorously — in the American colonies. Most British colonies blocked the entry of Catholic settlers. Nevertheless, special circumstances allowed for a tiny Catholic presence in colonial New York. There, worship could be conducted only privately and in near secrecy. Pennsylvania's openness in religious matters allowed a larger number of Catholics to settle there, exemplified in St. Joseph's Church in Philadelphia (1733), the first completely public Catholic parish in the British colonies. Before the Revolution, Catholics made up less than one percent of Pennsylvania's total population.

Maryland has a special place in Catholic history, for it was founded and initially ruled by a Catholic noble family, the Calverts, Barons of Baltimore. The first Lord Baltimore, having converted to Catholicism, began planning an American refuge for other English Catholics, who were not protected by high rank from the harsh anti-Catholic laws. In 1634, the ships *Ark* and *Dove* arrived in Chesapeake Bay, bringing Maryland's first colonists, a mixture of Catholics and Protestants. From the beginning, the Catholic proprietors knew that the colony could not succeed economically without encouraging non-Catholic settlers who would inevitably form the majority. Protestants were granted full religious rights, and eventually outnumbered Catholics more than ten to one. They took over the colony from the Catholic proprietors and applied the full force of British anti-Catholic laws to Catholics in Maryland. Despite severe persecution, including some executions, confiscation of Jesuit property, and prohibition of Catholic education and worship, Maryland Catholics were generally steadfast in their faith and remained the largest Catholic community in all the British colonies.

The revolutionary era found most American Catholics choosing the Patriot cause. Even though no one could say what the religious policy of the new nation would be, it was bound to be an improvement over the British laws. Catholics were further encouraged in their revolutionary sympathies when the two great Catholic powers, Spain and France, allied themselves with the United States in the War for Independence. And their hopes were fulfilled as the Constitution and Bill of Rights granted religious liberty to Catholics. State legislation, with some exceptions, conformed to the national decision. For the first time, Catholics enjoyed constitutional rights in a land that was overwhelmingly Protestant.

There was no central Catholic authority in the new nation. Thus, local groups of Catholics, especially outside of Maryland, began organizing themselves and securing priests wherever they could find them. This procedure was called "trusteeism," because the churches were governed by local trustees. Trusteeism helped launch Catholic congregations where no help could be offered by higher authority. But as traditional Catholic patterns of authority were established, the trustees often came into conflict with bishops and priests. These conflicts continued in some places until the Civil War.

A few years after the War for Independence, American priests were permitted to elect their first bishop. They chose John Carroll (1735-1815), a Jesuit priest and native Marylander, who was consecrated Bishop of Baltimore in 1790. Carroll found himself chief pastor of about thirty thousand Catholics, mostly in Maryland and Pennsylvania. When he became archbishop in 1808, the number had grown to seventy thousand, still about one percent of the American population. Gradually, scattered Catholics assumed the traditional patterns of support and authority, including bishops and duly appointed priests.

Perhaps the most serious problem that Carroll dealt with was the shortage of priests. To supplement the handful of American Jesuits and secular priests, Carroll accepted the support of the Society of St. Sulpice, centered in Paris.

Between 1791 and Carroll's death in 1815, nearly a hundred Sulpician priests arrived from France to labor in the United States. They founded a seminary and a college in Baltimore; several of them became bishops; and in other ways, they distinguished themselves in serving the infant church. Throughout the century, nuns, priests, and lay brothers from several other orders came from Germany, Belgium, France, Ireland, and elsewhere to help the American church. The first women's orders were French-derived houses of Carmelites and Ursulines, the latter maintaining schools in or around Baltimore, New Orleans, New York, and Boston. Elizabeth Bayley Seton (1774-1821), converted widow of a New York merchant, founded the first American order, the Sisters of Charity, in Maryland in 1809. Mother Seton was canonized in 1975 and is the church's first American-born saint.

By 1830, the church had eleven dioceses, over a dozen institutions of higher education, and hundreds of men and women under religious vows. The region between the Appalachians and the Mississippi had a growing Catholic population and was the scene of thriving parishes and missions. The dioceses of New Orleans and St. Louis, part of the Louisiana Purchase of 1803, had been to a large extent integrated into the American church. More than 200,000 Catholics made up around 1.6 percent of the American population. Impressive as these gains were, Catholicism in the United States was just beginning a century of almost unbelievable growth. At the end of this expansion, one quarter of all Americans would identify themselves as Catholics. The next four sections of this chapter deal with different aspects of that remarkable period from 1830 to 1925.

Immigration and Growth

The Catholic population would undoubtedly have lingered at one or two percent of the national population had it not been for changes in the pattern of immigration to this country. Unlike earlier immigrants, a large share of newcomers after 1820 were Catholic. Over a million Catholic immigrants arrived before 1850, around five million in the following half-century, and perhaps six million more between 1900 and 1925.

Arriving in large numbers after 1830, the Irish were the first national Catholic group to immigrate to America. As conditions in Ireland worsened during this period, a marked increase in immigration to America was the result.

The worst blow was the potato famine of the late 1840s. From 1846 to 1855, the Great Hunger killed a million and a half and sent more than a million fleeing to the United States. After that, the rate of Irish immigration began to decline, and continued in the background while other groups took the spotlight. A new German migration became significant in the 1840s, declined in the sixties, rose again after the Civil War, and tapered off before the end of the century. The total number of German immigrants surpassed the earlier tide of Irish. Some of the Germans were Protestant, some were Jewish, but the majority were Catholic. In the last twenty years of the nineteenth century, Catholics began arriving from southern and eastern Europe. Italians were the largest national group in this new migration. At the peak of their migration just before the First World War, two million Italians arrived in the United States in a single decade. From eastern Europe came representatives of many Catholic nationalities, including Hungarians, Lithuanians, Czechs, Slovaks, and Slovenians. But by far the largest group from that region were the Poles, who arrived in such numbers before the First World War that they became one of the "big four" among American Catholic nationalities, along with the Irish, the Germans, and the Italians.

Although some of the newcomers had emigrated because of political and religious problems, most of them were pushed from their old homes by economic pressure. In the same way, economic considerations largely determined where they settled in their new country. Most of the immigrants had backgrounds in farming, but relatively few of them succeeded in gaining a toehold in American agriculture. Various immigrant aid societies worked hard to settle the people new to this land, and the Germans were more successful in this effort than others. We think, too, of some Irish farming communities in the Middle West and of Italian and eastern European truck gardeners near the cities. But most of the Catholic immigrants from all nationalities usually found their livelihoods in the industrial towns and cities.

The century before the First World War was the century of America's industrial transformation: the nation needed millions of toiling bodies. Immigrants worked in slaughterhouses, factories, and quarries. They built canals and railroads, dug coal and metals, cut lumber, and made steel. They worked long hours under appalling conditions or alternately suffered stretches of forced unemployment. They reared their children in shanties and tenements. The Catholic Church served and grew in this immigrant world of poverty and anguish.

The organization of the church struggled to keep pace with the tide of immigration. By 1914, there were over a hundred dioceses covering the United States from coast to coast. The most populous dioceses were in the northeastern quadrant, where about three-quarters of American Catholics lived. Along with the erection of new dioceses came the extension of other Catholic institutions. For instance, by 1900 there were 827 Catholic charitable organizations. Virtually all of these were directed toward the assistance of distressed Catholics, reflecting the poverty of much of the church's membership.

Most remarkable was the institutional achievement reflected in the growth of a private educational system. Catholics were agreed that religious education had to be provided for all Catholic children, but they did not agree on how to do it. Many believed that Catholic needs could be met through some sort of shared time arrangement with the public schools. Such plans, however, were opposed by most Protestants and by many Catholics. The alternative was a whole separate system. In 1884, a council of bishops decreed that schools should be established in all parishes. Despite the decree, progress toward a full parochial system was slow, partly because of the modest resources available from rank-and-file Catholics. Nevertheless in 1914 parochial schools enrolled over a million pupils, taught by more than twenty thousand nuns. Even with these gains and the sacrifices they entailed, a large share of Catholic children were still being educated in public schools. Meanwhile, Catholic higher education was advancing. The Catholic University of America was opened in Washington in 1889, intended as a graduate institution to complement the strength of other institutions of higher learning, such as Georgetown, St. Louis, Fordham, Notre Dame, and Holy Cross.

A symbolic turning point was reached by American Catholicism in 1908. Up to that year the American church was under the care of the Congregation de Propaganda Fide in Rome, the worldwide Catholic mission agency. In 1908, Pope Pius X removed American Catholics from the jurisdiction of that agency. The church in the United States was no longer regarded as missionary territory but as equal to the European and Latin American churches. This declaration, long overdue in the opinion of many Catholics, expressed official recognition of the maturity and monumental achievement of Catholicism in this country. The church did not reach that point without conflict, however, both within its ranks and with its non-Catholic environment. We will look at the external conflict first.

Nativism and Anti-Catholicism

The lives of immigrants are never easy. Although they may find relief from the conditions that drove them from the old country, there is always a high price to pay. Catholic immigrants in the nineteenth century, like Jewish and Protestant newcomers in the same period, paid this price with the burdens of slum living, backbreaking labor, and the anguish of seeing their children depart from old-country customs. It is also true that they suffered the contempt and hurtful discrimination of the nativist movement.

In American history, "nativism" means anti-foreign agitation, particularly efforts to limit the number of immigrants and to suppress the political influence and civil rights of those who were already here. Nativists worked against all "foreigners," but Catholics were the focus of hostility during the nineteenth century. Reasons for nativist hostility were several. One was that immigrants clustered in the cities, and most Americans thought of cities as centers of sinful behavior. According to conventional wisdom, the cities were already bad, and the immigrants made them worse. Another reason was that immigrants were mostly industrial laborers at a time when the "respectable" occupations were thought to be in business or farming. Americans were not used to the idea of a huge wage-earning labor force. The idea frightened some. Then, too, there were protests from native workers who believed (sometimes correctly) that immigrant labor would harm them economically.

But Catholics were also the objects of a specifically religious hostility, in which nativism materialized as anti-Catholicism. One reason for this was the long history of combat between Catholics and Protestants — massacres, wars, executions — first in the name of religion and then in the name of national glory and wealth, but still with heavy religious overtones. Furthermore, Protestants and Catholics possessed false views of each other's religion. Each regarded the other as superstitious, immoral, and cruel.

Added to this was the fact that each of two branches of Christianity actually believed they were competing with each other for the souls of all Americans. We have seen that Protestant leaders imagined the ideal of America as a Protestant nation. As Catholic clergy gained confidence, they too dreamed aloud of the nation's religious future: America would be Catholic. Catholic gains, mostly through immigration, were impressive enough to alert and frighten many Protestants. One of the reasons that Protestants generously supported religious work in the Mississippi Valley was the belief that the Pope and the Catholic rulers of Europe were planning to take over the region, using the new immigrants as their agents. Many Protestants thought of the Pope himself as a "foreign ruler," to whom Catholics bore an allegiance. Naturally, it seemed to them, this religious allegiance would override an oath of allegiance to the United States. This led to a vein of hysteria in Protestant thought. Catholic churches were assumed to be centers of conspiracy and storehouses for guns and ammunition. For many Americans in 1840, the word "Catholic" carried the same thrill of horror as the word "Bolshevik" in 1920 or "Communist" in 1950.

With this climate of opinion in mind, we can imagine some of the results. Protestant periodicals began giving more space to anti-Catholic items, some restrained and others inflammatory. Books were published about the "papist conspiracy" and the supposed confessions of "escaped nuns." The most famous and durable of these was Maria Monk's *Awful Disclosures of the Hotel Dieu Nunnery of Montreal*, published 1836 and in several later editions. As a result of such fabrications and fantasies, many Americans believed that nuns existed mainly for the pleasure of priests, who visited them by means of secret tunnels, and that resulting infants were murdered and buried — if not dissolved in vats of acid — in the convent cellars.

Violence is also part of the anti-Catholic record. In 1834, a band of men carried out a careful plan to burn the Ursuline convent in suburban Boston. Although many Protestants expressed shock and denied responsibility, the tide of anti-Catholicism rolled on. In 1844, Philadelphia mobs, aided by militia, burned two Catholic churches and dozens of Irish homes, leaving thirteen dead and over fifty wounded. In New York, Bishop John Hughes, having determined that neither police nor militia would help protect Catholic lives and property, stationed bands of armed men around the churches and averted a repetition of the Philadelphia calamity.

These and smaller incidents in the 1840s were the climax of anti-Catholic violence. In the following decade, anti-Catholicism entered politics with the rise of the Order of the Star-Spangled Banner, popularly called the Know-Nothings. A combination of political party and secret lodge, they swore to oppose the election or appointment of Roman Catholics and foreigners to public office. Amazingly successful in local and state elections, by 1854 they won seventy-five congressional seats. But they lost influence rapidly after 1855, apparently because slavery became a more urgent political issue.

After the Civil War, political anti-Catholicism was revived, partly because of the new immigration from southern and eastern Europe and the increase of Catholic political power in northern cities. Many new lodges, political organizations, and veterans groups arose to nourish anti-Catholic sentiment. The most important of these was the American Protective Association, a middle western group formed in 1887. APA members were obligated not to vote for, strike with, or hire a Catholic. Although the APA was active in local campaigns, endorsing candidates and running a few of its own members, it was not a political party and did not achieve anything like the dazzling (if brief) success of the earlier Know-Nothings. Anti-Catholicism was losing some of its political appeal. At the same time, nativism in general was gaining decisive strength.

Vigorous as nativism was in the nineteenth century, its proponents could never muster the votes to restrict immigration. That situation changed near the turn of the century, as various kinds of nativist beliefs drew together. For instance, anti-Jewish sentiment began to appear along with anti-Catholicism. Also, new and popular racial theories declared that southern and eastern Europeans held an intermediate position between the "true" whites and the blacks. "Race suicide" and "reversion" would occur in America if more of these people were allowed to settle here and intermarry. Contributing to rising nativist influence were anti-labor and anti-radical opinions. Immigrants were deeply involved in labor's struggle for a voice in determining wages and working conditions. Sometimes they were animated by socialist ideas and sometimes not, but many Americans viewed all labor unrest as "radical." To restore tranquility, they thought, simply stop immigration. Ironically, the ranks of the nativists were increased by some children and grandchildren of immigrants, who took the position that further immigration was bad for the country. The First World War helped the nativist cause by increasing people's suspicion of all things foreign. After the war, the votes were there to change the nation's historic policy of free immigration. Among several restrictive measures, the act of 1924 was most important. Taking effect the following year, it established quotas for each national group, based on two percent of that group's presence in the population in 1890. This was designed to reduce the flow from southern and eastern Europe, the largest source of Catholic (and Jewish) immigrants at that time. The restriction of immigration, though arising partly from hostility to Catholics, indirectly benefited American Catholicism by permitting the church to become internally stronger and more unified.

Internal Problems

Any organization in a developing nation could expect to suffer a variety of problems and tensions. For the Roman Catholic Church, the normal problems were magnified, after 1830, by the arrival of thousands of new members every week. Rapid growth led to a severe and seemingly permanent shortage of priests. Consequently, former Catholics who settled in areas where there were few Catholics and no priests, would drift away from the church. Sometimes Catholics converted to Protestantism; more often they just abandoned all religious practice.

Internal problems were numerous. A series of skirmishes took place between bishops and local trustees. Another problem was how to respond to nativism. There was no lack of advice from Catholic leaders, but the advice pointed in different directions: overcome discrimination by showing your loyalty to American values; ignore the results and strengthen the walls of your ethnic enclave; defend yourself by force; avoid violence and pray for relief. The strategies were debated in Catholic neighborhoods and in Catholic hearts, and people made the best decisions they could.

It is interesting that the issue of slavery, which divided the nation and several of the Protestant denominations, did not divide the Catholic Church. Individual Catholics argued every degree of opinion, from absolute abolition to the staunchest defense of slavery, but the issue was not hotly debated in church councils. In fact, it was not really debated at all. The most scholarly Catholic writing on the subject was written in the 1840s by Bishop Francis Patrick Kenrick. He echoed the medieval Christian position that slavery was not necessarily bad either for the slave or the master. When the Civil War came, Catholics were found in both armies, but after the war the church quickly returned to normal, having no organizational wounds to heal.

Far more divisive than the issue of human slavery was the long series of battles over the role of separate nationalities in the church. Although Catholics were united in major features of belief and practice, they were separated by national custom and ethnic pride. In this sense, an Irish Catholic was not the same as a Polish Catholic. Holy days were celebrated differently, different saints' days were emphasized, and the languages of pulpit and confessional were different. At the local level, the problem might be solved by establishing parish boundaries to coincide with the ethnic neighborhoods and assigning priests of the same nationality. The situation grew more complex as some people insisted on having more bishops appointed from their group and demanded that certain parishes and schools be reserved for their nationality regardless of geographic considerations.

The shape of the ethnic struggle shifted more than once during the great century of Catholic immigration. We saw that early in the century priests came from France to serve the American church, though there were few French-descended people here. When the Irish began arriving in large numbers in the 1830s, they often found themselves served by French priests. We are not surprised that this arrangement did not work well; we are amazed that it worked at all. However, the situation changed. Irishmen entered the priesthood in unusually large numbers, despite the genteel contempt of the French and the few American-born priests. In a generation, the Irish took over, and the French (having no large ethnic constituency) faded from prominence. The Irish rose to leadership partly because they already spoke the language of their new country and partly because they were the first Catholic nationality to arrive in large numbers. For whatever reason, Irish preeminence in the American hierarchy continued, despite challenges, into the twentieth century; the majority of bishops today are of Irish descent.

The most vigorous nineteenth-century opponents of the Irish leadership were the German Catholics, whose main strength was in the Middle West, centering in Milwaukee, St. Louis, and Chicago. They had strong support from Catholic organizations in Germany and were able to influence some decisions in Rome. Could the Irish priests and bishops maintain a strong, true Catholicism in the United States? Many were convinced and made their opinions known through a loud, emphatic "no." They believed that only through the tradition of German learning and loyalty (communicated, of course, in the German language) could true Christianity be maintained against the hostile Protestant majority. In every way possible, they struggled to establish an enclave of German Catholicism, including parishes, schools, seminaries, and religious orders, culturally self-sufficient and distinct from other nationalities. They partly succeeded: for instance, in certain places the bishop was always a man of German descent. But their grand design failed, in part because of strong opposition within the church. But, finally, the plan failed because of the fanatical anti-Germanism of the First World War, and the subsequent move on the part of many German-Americans to loosen their attachment to their heritage and become "100% American."

Poles and Italians and other ethnic groups also struggled for, and sometimes achieved, a measure of ethnic autonomy in some localities. What was achieved, however, did not always satisfy. One dispute involving Polish immigrants against Irish bishops resulted in a separation from the Roman Church. In 1907, the separatist Polish National Church was formed and endures to this day, with over 250,000 members.

One more dispute or cluster of disputes occurred in the closing years of the nineteenth century. The issue was the attitude of American Catholics to American society and government. The factions may be labeled conservatives and liberals, if we understand that the terms do not refer to theological issues (as with Protestants in the same period) but to questions of church and state, and interfaith relations. The conservatives, probably the majority of clergy and laity, believed that America was a religiously dangerous place for Catholics. Society was not really neutral but Protestant-oriented, and Catholics should keep to themselves as much as possible, lest they be seduced or coerced away from the true faith. On the other side were the liberals — sometimes called Americanists, though they did not accept the term — who believed that America offered a unique opportunity to Catholics to leave behind the church-state problems of the European churches. It was a chance to create a purer form of Catholicism. Therefore, the proper course was to be open to the currents of American life, including contact with non-Catholics. This would not only strengthen one's own faith but attract new converts as well.

In the background of this disagreement was the life and work of Father Isaac Hecker (1819-1888), who died before the controversy reached its climax. He was a pioneer of the liberal position. An American-born convert from Protestantism, Hecker founded an order of missionary priests, the Paulist Fathers, whose aim was to win converts from the non-Catholic population of the United States. Hecker and the Paulists publicized Catholicism as the best answer to the spiritual problems of citizens in a democratic society. At the same time, they portrayed America as a healthy environment for Catholicism. In other words, Hecker was optimistic about America rather than fearful and guarded. He influenced not only the priests of his own order but also many other clergymen, who later formed the core of the liberal or Americanist faction. Conservatives, on the other hand, believed that Hecker and his admirers glossed over essential differences between Catholicism and the Protestant heresies, gave too much room for individual experience, and wanted to make the American church something different from the true universal Catholic Church.

Tensions between liberals and conservatives produced many episodes. A fight preceded the founding of the Catholic University of America. Liberals wanted it as a proving ground for Catholic education in modern America, while conservatives opposed it as a center of dangerous thinking. Dissent continued in other areas of education as well. While some liberals wanted to conduct Catholic education in cooperation with public schools, conservatives insisted on a full system of private schools. Another issue surrounded the Knights of Labor. This early labor union had some features of a secret society of the kind opposed by the Catholic Church. Although American conservatives wanted the Pope to condemn the Knights, liberals succeeded in persuading the Vatican that the organization no longer required a secret oath, that it was not socialist, and that it was of great benefit to the Catholic poor. Despite the liberal success in this case, official Vatican statements of 1895 and 1899 did much to discourage the liberal faction and to weaken their cause. Another kind of Catholic liberalism appeared in the 1920s, but Hecker's type of concern for the church in modern society did not re-emerge until 1958 with the pontificate of John XXIII.

Strengthening Parish Life

When we speak of "Catholic" immigrants, we are, of course, talking about people with various degrees of religious commitment. Choice or circumstance dictated that some of them would have only the slightest connection with religious practice. Many performed only the minimum obligations prescribed by Catholic teaching. Others were Catholic only in the sense that they had been baptized as infants and belonged to an ethnic group in which Catholicism was the only recognized form of religion. They were seen in church only for the weddings and the funerals of their friends.

From the viewpoint of the clergy and the more committed laity, such fringe Catholics were not part of the church's support but part of its burden: an internal mission field. We saw that Protestants had a similar internal mission field, made up of uncommitted persons of Protestant background, and they used revival meetings to deal with it. Catholics also had revivals, often called parish missions or parish retreats. These Catholic revivals were geared for reclaiming lapsed members and strengthening the faithful. Recent research of Jay P. Dolan (see Bibliography) reveals much about these nineteenth-century missions. The following description is based on his work.

The parish mission had its roots in the work of itinerant friar-priests in the high middle ages. Its greatest popularity was in the latter half of the nineteenth century. In Italy, France, Germany, and Britain, the parish mission was one feature of a general renewal of Catholic devotion during that period. In the United States, the majority of bishops quickly gave their support to the idea, and several religious orders began giving special attention to it. As a result, thousands of missions were conducted in America between 1850 and the end of the century. The orders most active in this effort were the Redemptorists, the Jesuits, the Passionists, the Dominicans, and Hecker's Paulists. These organizations selected and trained special bands of priest-missioners, whose only work was to travel from place to place conducting parish missions. In this way, all regions of the nation were influenced by this powerful religious technique. Although rural parishes were not neglected, the large Catholic populations of the urban parishes understandably received more frequent attention.

In consultation with the team of missioners, the pastor of the parish determined when to hold the mission. This was usually planned to last for one or two weeks, though sometimes for as long as a month. By the latter part of the century, various orders had published handbooks to guide missioners and parish priests in conducting the mission. As with Protestant revivals, all available media were used to publicize the event: announcements at Mass, house to house visits by parish clergy, newspaper advertisements, posters, banners, handbills, and leaflets. One leaflet explained the mission and urged attendance in these terms:

> *It is a time when the greatest truths of religion are preached to you. It is a time when priests from early morning till night wait in the confessional for you. . . . It is a time when all things are made most easy and favorable to you to save that soul which will live on after your body is dead, and never die.*

Choirs and bands were rehearsed; a platform and large

cross were constructed; stocks of religious books and devotional items — rosaries, crucifixes, medals, pictures, scapulars — were ordered. Scores of details were looked after in preparation for the big event.

A mission normally began with Sunday morning High Mass and sermon. Between Sundays, each day of the mission began with five o'clock Mass and a brief instructional talk, so that working people could conveniently get to breakfast and arrive at their jobs on time. A mid-morning Mass and instruction followed, then an early evening instruction and rosary, and finally an hour-long sermon followed by a closing act of devotion, such as the Benediction of the Holy Eucharist. Music was important in establishing the mood of the mission, as were various rituals; these were adopted by the missioners especially for the occasions. But for many people, the most memorable features of the missions were the special sermons delivered each night.

Above all other talents, missioners were supposed to be gifted preachers. The mission sermon was planned to move the hearts and minds of the hearers toward contrition and "friendship with God." Because of certain doctrinal and cultural features, Catholic and Protestant revival sermons were not identical, but they were very similar in rhetorical device and emotional impact. Walter Elliott, a Paulist missioner, wrote that "the mission sermon ought to be a masterpiece, arousing the emotions of fear, reverence, awe, hatred of sin, and the love of God." The Jesuit Arnold Damen, a huge man with a booming voice, was one of the most effective mission preachers. Holding aloft in the pulpit a large crucifix, he would sometimes address the Savior:

> *My God, it was my sins of wantonness and rebellion, leading me to occasions of sin, that caused those fearful wounds in your sacred Feet; my refusal to walk to Sunday Mass drove the nails deeper and deeper; my cursing, swearing, my uncharitable and blasphemous speech that caused the awful parching of your sacred lips.*

Redemptorist preacher Joseph Wissel, though he counseled other preachers not to try to make people weep, was known for his ability to do that very thing. Sometimes when people began crying during his sermons, he made the most of it by saying, "Don't cry now but cry at your confession: then bewail your sins."

All revivalists want people to do something to symbolize and confirm their change of heart. In the case of Catholic missions, the goal was to draw people to the confessional and then to Holy Communion. Beginning on the third or fourth day of the mission, extra priests were on hand to staff the confessionals from early morning till late at night. During a successful mission, people waited in line at all hours to receive the sacrament of Penance. For some people, this would be the first confession in many years, a turning point in their lives, a return to the state of grace.

Assessing the results of decades of missions, there is no doubt that Catholicism was greatly benefited by the effort. Diverse and conflicting factions within the church agreed about the value of parish missions and cooperated in making them effective. Tensions between conservatives and liberals and between ethnic groups were reduced by the parish mission campaign. Many negligent Catholics drew closer to the church, while the faithful were confirmed in their faithfulness. Before the turn of the century, the Paulists and some others began conducting missions to non-Catholics, resulting in some conversions.

After The "Great War"

The years between the World Wars brought internal strengthening and adjustment to American Catholicism. Restrictive immigration ended a hundred-year period of staggering growth. Although the restrictions were motivated partly by anti-Catholicism, many Catholic leaders agreed that most problems were easier to handle without the flood of immigrants. Indeed, some problems seemed to solve themselves as the percentage of American-born Catholics steadily increased.

For one thing, disputes between nationalities declined, partly because native-born Catholics were largely unmoved by the feelings that stirred their immigrant parents or grandparents. And as time went on the immigrants themselves were reassured that their "American" children were growing up with a firm Catholic loyalty even in the absence of the supposed protection of ethnic isolation. Ethnic solidarity became more and more a matter of social preference rather than religious urgency. As the boundaries between ethnic groups softened, religious solidarity remained very strong. Most Catholics thought it important to associate mainly with other Catholics and to give generously for schools, missions, and other churchly needs.

From the outside, nativist pressures, though still strong during the twenties, diminished at an accelerating rate in the thirties and forties. Charges of disloyalty, always a big item in the nativist attack, were countered by the large proportion of young Catholics in the wartime army of 1917-1918. The Secretary of War estimated that thirty-five percent of new recruits were Catholics, even though at that time less than twenty percent of the general population were of that faith. In political and economic life, Catholics often made common cause with non-Catholics, thus fostering interfaith toleration. Also, they were generally opposed to socialism and communism in politics and economics, which turned aside the nativist attack against "foreign radicals." At the level of daily contacts, more and more Catholics looked and sounded "American" rather than "foreign." However, it was during the Second World War (1941-1945) that most people came to accept the idea of "three great faiths." In the armed forces, it was equally acceptable to be a Protestant, Catholic, or Jew. Stories and articles made much of the friendly cooperation and equal heroism of the warriors of all three religions. By the end of the war, anti-Catholic feelings had become politically and socially insignificant.

Increasing internal and external harmony helped bring forth new strength and confidence. Among the signs was a reversal in the relationship of the American church to foreign missions. For over a hundred years, American Catholics had received foreign aid, both in terms of money and personnel. By 1918, American Catholics were ready to send people and dollars overseas to blaze new trails for the faith. In that year, four priests of the Catholic Foreign Missionary Society of America (informally called Maryknoll) departed for service in China. Financial support increased rapidly, until over half of the Catholic missions in the world were supported by contributions from the United States.

Another sign of internal strength was the formation of the National Catholic Welfare Conference. Successor of a wartime organization, the N.C.W.C., from the twenties onward, consisted of a research and program staff for the American bishops, who collectively ruled the church. The N.C.W.C comprised several departments — originally Education, Lay Activities, Press, Social Action, and Missions. Each made recommendations for the bishops to consider and, often, to approve. The effect was to unify the official Catholic viewpoint on certain issues. An example was the document known as "The Bishops' Program of Social Reconstruction," written in 1919 by Monsignor John A. Ryan (1869-1945), head of the N.C.W.C.'s Social Action Department. The statement favored the minimum wage, labor's right to organize and bargain, public housing, a national employment service, laws against child labor, as well as insurance benefits for the elderly, the unemployed, and the victims of industrial accidents. This program, similar to proposals by Protestants of the Social Gospel movement, was not popular during the prosperous twenties, even among most Catholics. But in the Great Depression of the thirties, such proposals made sense to millions of Americans. Under Franklin Roosevelt's New Deal, most of the items in the "Bishops' Program" became national policy.

Another sign of growing maturity was the rise of the liturgical movement. The word *liturgy* refers to the church's acts of collective worship, especially the Mass, which Catholics believe is the reenactment of Christ's sacrifice on the cross. The liturgical movement consisted of people who wanted, among other aims, to foster greater understanding of the Mass and to increase intelligent participation in it. Many Catholics in the twenties attended Mass as a mere obligation without knowing what they were doing. Others used the time spent at Mass to perform private devotions, such as the Rosary, that had no direct connection with the words and acts of the Mass itself. There were reasons why so many loyal Catholics paid little attention to the substance of the Mass: it was conducted in Latin, which few understood; it consisted of a swift sequence of symbolic words and actions, whose meaning required explanation; and ordinary Catholics thought of it as something done for them by the priest without requiring their active participation. Leaders of the liturgical movement mounted an educational effort aimed at priests, parish teachers, and laypeople. As a result, priests and teachers began giving more and better instruction about the significance of the Mass and the meaning of its various parts. Many parishes introduced the dialogue Mass, in which the assembled worshipers recite some of the prayers. An indication of the success of these efforts was the growing popularity of new editions of the Missal. These Missals contained the full text of the Mass, usually with Latin and English versions side by side, together with illustrations and explanations of the priest's action. The use of the new Missals increased from a few thousands in the twenties to many millions in the fifties.

Another indication of new strength among American Catholics was their participation in the political and economic life of the nation. Catholic political power, established first in the northeastern cities, gradually expanded into state and local governments. Forces for and against Catholic political participation focused on the presidential campaign of 1928, in which the Democrats nominated a Catholic candidate,

New York's popular governor, Alfred E. Smith. Some the votes that sent Herbert Hoover to the White House were motivated by anti-Catholicism, especially in some of the normally Democratic southern states. On the other hand, there were a number of other issues favoring Hoover, including eight years of prosperity under Republican presidents. Although Smith lost by a landslide, he gathered more votes than any other postwar Democratic presidential candidate. Furthermore, the forces generated by his campaign, including the marshalling of the Catholic vote, prepared the way for the Democrats' victory in 1932.

Catholic economic activity naturally focused on the labor movement, because so many Catholics were industrial workers. The chief goal of labor's struggle in the postwar years was to win the right to organize unions and to bargain collectively. In the twenties, most Americans, including many Catholics, thought that collective bargaining was unAmerican. It would destroy private business and subvert democracy. Despite the "Bishops' Program," Catholic businessmen and many priests opposed the efforts of pro-union Catholic workers. The tide turned with the coming of the New Deal, when industrial unions gained a solid legal foundation. Among the Catholic groups supporting this development was the Association of Catholic Trade Unionists, founded in 1937 to help Catholics function as effective union members and leaders. In the thirties, a third or more of all union members were Catholic. One of the Catholic influences upon the union movement was to help slant it toward non-political, bread-and-butter objectives. Radical politics, so much a part of the European labor movement, were not generally favored by American workers. The goals of American labor, with its large segment of loyal Catholics, were comfortably contained within capitalist economics and two-party politics.

The Winds of Change

The two decades after the Second World War carried American Catholicism far beyond its origins as a tiny struggling minority and its adolescence as a burgeoning immigrant church. During the fifties, Catholics enjoyed a new status, certified by their war service, as one of the nation's "three great faiths." They joined the movement to the suburbs and benefited proportionally from postwar prosperity and expanded educational opportunities. The majority of Catholics were at home in a country that was indeed their own. And the grand symbol of their new, altered status was the election of President John Fitzgerald Kennedy, showing that Catholic religion was no barrier to even the nation's highest honor.

We recall that the fifties brought a "revival of religion" in this country, marked outwardly by increases in attendance at worship, financial contributions, educational programs, and church construction, among other phenomena. Catholics shared this surge of religious feeling and affiliation. Particularly, they established hundreds of new suburban parishes. Beneath the surface of expansion and achievement, however, some Catholics were warning of the shortcomings of the American church. They pointed to the defensive "fortress" mentality of many priests and laypeople, to the dominance of the clergy and the passivity of the laity in church life, and to the rigid and often mechanical quality of Catholic instruction, particularly moral instruction. This kind of self-criticism and internal debate is in itself a sign of health and maturity. In the mid-fifties, however, no one could have guessed that the voices for change would be joined by the voice of the Pope himself.

Late in 1958, Angelo Guiseppe Roncalli (1881-1963) became Pope John XXIII. Compassionate, humble, and humorous, Pope John became the most beloved pontiff of modern times, winning the admiration of non-Catholics as well as Catholics. Despite his advanced age, his brief pontificate was vigorous and far-sighted. He managed to gather the forces of reform and renewal into a remarkably successful effort to bring the church up to date. His most important act was to call the Second Vatican Council, which met in several sessions from 1962 to 1965. (The later sessions were led by Pope Paul VI after John's death in 1963.)

American Catholics became deeply involved in "Pope John's Revolution," notably in the areas of worship and interfaith relations. Latin nearly disappeared from Catholic worship, as the English (or Spanish) Mass became the norm in the United States. In many churches the altar was moved away from the wall, so that the priest could celebrate Mass while facing the people. As in Protestant churches, hymn-singing became an important feature of worship. Guitars and wind instruments sometimes accompanies the singing. Laypeople rather than priests stood at the lectern to read the Bible to the congregation. Many people disapproved of these changes. Catholic worship is still developing in an atmosphere of discussion and experimentation. It is likely that changes in worship partly account for a decrease in attendance at Mass since 1960.

Vatican II also facilitated a new Catholic attitude toward other religions, notably Orthodox and Protestant Christians as well as Jews. When Pope John referred to Protestants as "our separated brethren," Catholics in the United States could feel the ice melt. Priests were free to participate with Jews, Protestants, and Orthodox in public events and even to preach in non-Catholic worship services. Important Catholic publications emphasized interfaith cooperations and dialogue, and the American bishops established the Committee for Ecumenical and Interreligious Affairs. Serious discussion of doctrinal differences proceeded in the new atmosphere of friendliness.

On the other hand, the years since Pope John and Vatican II have also brought Catholics to a crisis of authority. Many Catholics, priests as well as laypeople, disagree with the traditionally authoritarian style of Catholic church administration. For these people, "authority" has become a doubtful term, and words like "dialogue," "conscience," and even "democracy" have become important in describing a desired style of decision-making. An important issue in this regard is contraception. Most recent studies show that Catholics, including the ones who attend Mass most regularly, practice birth control at about the same rate as non-Catholics. Many priests at least tacitly approve of family planning, including the use of "artificial" methods. Yet both Pope Paul VI in 1968 and Pope John Paul II during his visit to the United States in 1979 strongly reasserted the traditional Catholic opposition to "contraceptive acts." Such pronouncements, while pleasing to many Catholics, leave others troubled and angry. Conflicts of this kind increase the burden not only upon families but upon parish priests. The priesthood is evidently not as attractive to young men as it once was. The number of seminarians declined from 49,000 in 1965 to 11,200 in 1978.

Thus the Catholic Church in the United States enters the 1980s with a mixture of worry and hope. General loyalty has visibly declined, and Catholics disagree — sometimes bitterly — over several important matters. But at the same time, many Catholics are displaying new levels of religious creativity and commitment. Some people believe that the church faces the greatest hazards and greatest opportunities in its history during the final decades of the twentieth century.

Selected People and Events

1565 Establishment of the first Catholic parish within the limits of the future United States of America at St. Augustine, Florida.

1622 Congregation de Propoganda Fide is established in Rome with jurisdiction over Catholics in America and other mission fields.

1634 Arrival of the first Catholic settlers in Maryland.

1649 Enactment of Maryland's law of religious toleration, repealed in 1654.

1673 Louis Joliet and Father Jacques Marquette explore the Mississippi.

1687 Eusebio Kino (1644-1711), a Jesuit priest, begins missions in Arizona.

1727 Ursuline Sisters arrive from France to open the first Catholic school in New Orleans.

1769 Junipero Serra (1713-1784), a Franciscan priest, begins missions in California.

1776 Virginia becomes the first state to vote full religious freedom in its bill of rights.

1789 Inauguration of the first national administration under the Constitution and Bill of Rights. The beginning of religious freedom at the national level.

1790 John Carroll (1735-1815) is consecrated Bishop of Baltimore, the first bishop in the United States. Becomes the first archbishop in 1808.

1791 Sulpician priests from France establish the first Catholic seminary in the United States.

1809 Elizabeth Bayley Seton (1774-1821) founds the Sisters of Charity, the first native religious order. In 1975, Mother Seton becomes the first American-born saint.

1820 John England (1786-1842) arrives from Ireland to become Bishop of Charleston, South Carolina. Establishes the first U.S. Catholic newspaper in 1822. He is remembered for pioneering efforts in education, administration, and interfaith relations.

1834 Nativists burn the Ursuline convent in Charlestown, Massachusetts.

1844 Nativist riots in Philadelphia leave thirteen dead.

1858 Isaac Hecker (1819-1888) establishes the Paulist Fathers, the first native religious order for men.

1869 Forty-nine American bishops attend the First Vatican Council.

1875 Archbishop John McCloskey (1810-1885) becomes the first American cardinal.

1887 Archbishop James Gibbons (1834-1921) becomes the second American cardinal, and an important "Americanist" leader, along with Archbishop John Ireland (1838-1918), Bishop John Keane (1839-1918), and Monsignor Denis O'Connell (1849-1927).

1889 Opening of the Catholic University of America in Washington, with Bishop Keane as the first rector.

1893 Opening in Baltimore of the first U.S. Catholic college for women, the College of Notre Dame of Maryland.

1908 U.S. Catholic Church is removed from the list of mission fields under the jurisdiction of the Congregation de Propaganda Fide in Rome.

1911 Establishment of the Catholic Foreign Mission Society of America (Maryknoll), which sent out first American Catholic missionaries in 1918.

1919 Publication of the "Bishops' Program of Social Reconstruction" by the Social Action Department of the National Catholic Welfare Conference.

1921 Congress passes the first of the immigration laws based on nationality quotas. By 1925, stricter laws curtailed Catholic growth from overseas.

1928 Alfred E. Smith, the first Catholic presidential candidate of a major party, is defeated by Herbert C. Hoover.

1930 Fulton John Sheen (1895-1979), philosophy professor and after 1951 a bishop, broadcasts his first "Catholic Hour" radio program, beginning long service as an influential radio and television preacher.

1932 Franklin Roosevelt is elected president by a new Democratic coalition that includes nearly all Catholic voters.

1933 The first issue of the *Catholic Worker* is published by Dorothy Day (b. 1897), leader of a movement combining deep Catholic piety with vigorous action on behalf of the poor.

1937 Founding of the Assocation of Catholic Trade Unionists.

1941 U.S. enters the Second World War, resulting in a rapid decline of anti-Catholic feeling.

1958 Election of Pope John XXIII.

1960 Election of John Fitzgerald Kennedy, the first Catholic president of the United States.

1962 The first session of the Second Vatican Council, called by Pope John.

1968 Pope Paul VI issues his encyclical *Humanae Vitae* (Of Human Life) dealing with sexuality and including a reiteration of the ban on contraception; several American theologians publicly dissent.

1978 The "year of three popes," including the death of Paul VI and John Paul I as well as the election of John Paul II.

1979 Pope John Paul II visits the United States, addressing large audiences in several cities.

CHAPTER SIX

Judaism: New Promise and New Exodus

Jews are the largest non-Christian group in the United States, making up over 3 percent of the American population. This country has the largest Jewish population of any nation in the world, with the State of Israel second and the Soviet Union third.

In many respects, the growth of the Jewish population parallels that of the Catholics, but at a slower rate. After the Revolution only about one American in a thousand was a Jew. Then, after 1836, the German migration, which brought so many Catholics to this country, also increased the Jewish population to one in a hundred Americans by 1880. But the greatest number of Jewish immigrants came from eastern Europe beginning in the 1880s, along with Catholics from the same region. When that migration slowed to a trickle in 1925, nearly 4 percent of all Americans were Jews.

Colonial Beginnings: The Sefardim

The territory of the future United States received its first Jews in 1654. They arrived in the Dutch colony of New Amsterdam, which was renamed New York ten years later, after being taken by the British. These and most other Jews of the colonial period were Sefardim by descent and tradition. The designation Sefardim or Sefardic Jews referred to Jews who lived in Spain and Portugal in the Middle Ages and to their descendants who migrated elsewhere. The name distinguishes them from the Ashkenazim, who lived in northern Europe in the Middle Ages and whose descendants eventually made up the bulk of American Jewry.

Judaism.
116

Under Muslim rule in Spain and Portugal beginning in the eighth century, the Sefardic Jews established a generally prosperous and peaceful life. This situation deteriorated as Christian rulers gradually reconquered the Iberian Peninsula. Systematic persecution became the order of the day until the Christian sovereigns of Spain (1492) and Portugal (1496) expelled the large Jewish populations from their domains. Some escaped the decrees by converting or pretending to convert to Catholicism. Others fled to North Africa and Turkey, while some found refuge in Holland, especially the city of Amsterdam, at a time when most parts of western Europe were closed to Jews. From Holland, some Jewish families moved to Dutch colonies in the Americas. Thus a century and a half after the expulsion, some Portuguese Sefardim arrived in New Amsterdam. Later they gained permission for public worship and formed the first North American synagogue, Shearith Israel (Remnant of Israel).

Meanwhile, other Sefardic immigrants arrived in other cities of the British mainland colonies: Newport, Charleston, Savannah, Richmond, and Philadelphia. In worship, these people followed the dignified tradition of medieval Spain. In matters of business and daily living they freely associated with the non-Jewish majority. Some of them became part of the growing class of well-to-do colonial merchants. They had no rabbis in the colonial period, but strong leadership was often provided by cantors. These men qualified themselves by training and practice to lead the chanting of the synagogue services. They were usually amateurs or semi-professionals, earning most of their living by other work. Later, in the absence of ordained rabbis, they sometimes became paid "ministers" of synagogues.

After 1830, the Sefardim became numerically insignificant compared to waves of German and eastern European

Ashkenazim. They formed a cultured aristocracy in the half-dozen oldest synagogues in the country. Eventually, they lost their distinctive identity among Americans except in the proud traditions of certain old families.

German Immigrants and The Rise of Reform Judaism

Beginning in 1836, large groups of Jews began immigrating from Germany and other German-speaking areas of Central Europe. When the migration ended a half-century later, about 200,000 of them had arrived in this country. In Germany, most Jews in this period were still subject to special laws designed to destroy Jewish business competition and even to limit Jewish population. For instance, Bavarian laws restricted the number of Jewish marriages. When these and other disabilities reached a critical level, significant mass migration from Germany began, with Bavarian Jews leading the way.

Most of the newcomers were very poor, bringing little capital and no important business connections. Occupationally, they were craftsmen or retail traders of the humbler sort: tinkers, cobblers, pack-peddlers, pawnbrokers, and others of similar status. Having been barred for centuries from agriculture in Europe, they did not think of becoming farmers in America, as so many others did. Rather, their background taught them to look for opportunities in retail trading, often of the lowliest kind. True, the difference in language was a formidable obstacle at first, but it was quickly overcome in the face of immense opportunities. Jews discovered that Americans, despite a certain suspicion of foreigners, had no laws directed specifically against Jews. Jewish individuals, families, and communities could function very much like other Americans. Economically, there were hardly any of the regulations, licenses, taxes, and other harassments that brought misery to the lives of small tradesmen in Germany.

These conditions determined the livelihoods of the majority of the German immigrants and their children. Although some of them stayed in New York and other eastern cities, the majority fanned out to serve as storekeepers to the westward moving population. Columbus, Birmingham, Little Rock, Des Moines, Independence, Denver, Sante Fe, Sacramento, and hundreds of smaller places became home for the German Jews. Sometimes Jews would be among the first white settlers in a new location. This is why Cincinnati became an important center for educating rabbis and why

San Francisco had a small Jewish congregation as early as 1849. The Jewish peddler was a familiar sight on forest paths and country roads. The general store in the prairie village or the mining camp would very likely be operated by a partnership of German Jews. The work was hard and often dangerous. Many fragile businesses failed, but many others succeeded, eventually growing into department stores and dry goods stores.

The cost of economic success, however, included social isolation and religious instability. In order to understand the religious development of German Jews in this country, it is helpful to look first at the European development and background.

Judaism in Germany. In the nineteenth century, before mid-century at least, most Jews in Germany still honored and observed the centuries-old traditions contained in the Talmud and the prayer book and interpreted by traditionally oriented rabbis. The Talmud is a body of Judaic teaching compiled between 200 and 600, which became the basis for the faith and practice of the majority of the world's Jews. It was regarded as Oral Torah, revealed along with the written Torah to Moses on Mount Sinai. This multi-volume work deals with all aspects of life: Sabbath observance, holy days, diet, marriage, contracts, civil damages, crimes, and other matters. Wherever possible Jews secured permission from Christian officials to regulate their affairs according to their own talmudic laws. In addition, there were certain customs, such as covering the head during prayer, that had the force of divine law, even though they were not prescribed in the Talmud or the Bible.

The Jewish tradition required certain fixed forms of prayer three times daily, with additions and variations for Sabbath and holy day services. These forms of prayer are contained in the traditional prayer book in the Hebrew language, divided into the *siddur*, comprising the daily prayers, and the *mazhor*, containing the prayers for holy days. Morning, afternoon, and evening, the observant Jew recited the prayers that had been recited by generations of Jews stretching back to ancient times. In the mornings and on certain evenings, Jews preferred to pray in a congregation rather than alone. This required a *minyan*, a quorum or minimum gathering, of ten men. Women were not counted for the minyan. So German shopkeepers, peddlers, craftsmen, and laborers often arose in the morning and hurried to the synagogue. If the town had few Jews, there would be anxiety about whether enough men would arrive to constitute a minyan. Certain portions of the daily prayers could only be offered "in congregation," being omitted by individuals and groups smaller than ten.

Traditional rabbis were primarily teachers and interpreters of talmudic law. This primary function carried them into the roles of advisor, judge, and scholar within the confines of Jewish communities. It is noteworthy that traditional rabbis were not normally leaders of worship or preachers of sermons. The men took turns leading worship or assigned the function to a regular cantor, while sermons or lectures were not a regular feature of Jewish worship.

Even though most German Jews were loyal to the tradition of Talmud, prayer book, and rabbi, important changes were taking place in the nineteenth century. For one thing, by this time German states normally refused to permit Jews to apply talmudic law to important areas of life. Crimes, contracts, damages, and marriages, among other matters, were regulated by German law, often (as we saw) with unfavorable attention to Jews. Thus, the Talmud lost its relevance in many situations. Furthermore, economic and social turmoil had a disintegrating effect on Jewish communities, resulting in poorer education and less understanding of the Jewish tradition. Even the prayers lost their meaning for those people who did not learn to read Hebrew adequately. Wherever the tradition was eroded the authority of the traditional rabbi also declined.

The developments just described affected Jews of low and middle class status in most regions of Germany. In addition, another kind of change arose among small groups of well-educated, prosperous Jews in certain German cities, such as Hamburg. They were eager to "reform" the Jewish tradition, so that its enduring values might be more obvious to the non-Jewish majority. That meant shedding those features of Jewish life that "Reform" Jews believed were irrelevant to essential Judaism and offensive to their Christian neighbors. They denied the authority of the Talmud while affirming the authority of the Scriptures. The dietary laws, even those enjoined in the Bible, were discarded. Prayers were conducted in German. The rabbis were expected to deliver sermons, much like the neighboring Protestant ministers. Organs and choirs made their appearance in the synagogues. Synagogue music sounded like the Bach chorales in the Lutheran churches nearby. Men and women were seated together in family groups. These anti-traditional practices affected a rather small part of the Jewish population in the early nineteenth century, but that part produced a relatively large number of new-style rabbis, university-trained in history and philosophy, and full of ideas about Reform Judaism. Some of them moved to the United States.

Religious Conditions In The United States. Jews in the

early years of the German migration to America experienced general religious disorganization. In the larger cities, they could establish sizable synagogues, but these congregations were often uncertain about proper Jewish practice in the new land. Those many Jews scattered in a thousand towns and villages across the country were in a worse religious situation. Many lived where it was impossible to gather a minyan for worship, let alone provide religious training for their children. Many immigrants, though perhaps wishing to be loyal to tradition, found themselves lacking knowledge to follow it in the new environment with an absence of authoritative guidance. Jews were virtually without any type of rabbis until the 1840s, and the number was much too small for many years afterward. Traditional Jews did not require a rabbi to lead worship, but they did need one for instruction and counsel.

Other factors also contributed to religious uncertainty among German-American Jews. Religious freedom meant that people were free to practice Judaism any way they wished or to avoid religious practice altogether. They could even shed their Jewish identity completely without converting to Christianity. In this situation, there was no barrier to creating non-traditional forms of Judaism, if such practices found support among the people. And they were bound to find favor with those Jews whose ties with the tradition were weakened by the lack of guidance and by daily contact with the Christian majority. Such people might understandably welcome a form of Judaism that would not distinguish them too obviously from their non-Jewish neighbors. This was the condition of much of the German Jewish population when the first rabbis arrived from Germany.

The Beginnings of American Reform Judaism. It is an important fact that all of the earliest rabbis in America were men influenced by German Reform Judaism. By virtue of their education and rabbinical ordination, they could claim superior authority in interpreting Jewish life and worship. Of course, they had to persuade their constituents that the claim was valid and their ideas were sound. In a remarkably brief time they moved the majority of German Jews in the direction of Reform.

The movement, of course, occupied the energies of many men and women, but if we were to pick one key figure in the rise of American Reform, it would be Isaac Meyer Wise. From the time he arrived in the United States in 1846, at the age of twenty-seven, until his death in 1900, he seemed constantly engaged in reforming, organizing, and Americanizing the Jewish population. His reforming efforts split his first congregation in Albany into modern and traditional groups. In 1854, he became rabbi of a congregation in Cincinnati, and in the same year he founded an English-language weekly newspaper, the *American Israelite*. Three years later, he published the first edition of a modernized prayer book, which passed through several editions and gradually found favor among the growing number of Reform-minded congregations. In 1873, after conferences with other rabbis, Wise founded the Union of American Hebrew Congregations, which is still the main association of Reform congregations. Two years later, he opened Hebrew Union College in Cincinnati, the first durable Jewish institution of higher learning in the United States. Its principal mission was to train American rabbis.

By that time, there were nearly two hundred major Jewish congregations, serving a Jewish population of a quarter-million. All but a few of them had departed visibly from traditional Judaism, that is, they were "reformed" in various degrees. Some followed the practice of Reform synagogues in Germany by calling their houses of worship "temples." Reform worship was conducted in a manner very different from traditional worship (Glazer, 46).

> *The service was no longer read and sung by the congregation but read by the minister. Almost all of it was now in English. The congregation participated only in responsive readings and a hymn or two. Hats and prayer shawls were removed. An organ and a choir were introduced, and the choir usually included men and women instead of men and boys as in Orthodox practice. The balcony on which women sat, out of sight of the men, was removed, and men and women sat together. Some congregations even adopted a Sunday service. The main feature of the service became the sermon.*

Reform worship thus became similar to middle-class Protestant worship with the rabbi as minister. However, the Sunday services were not well attended, and Friday evening became the main worship time for most Reform Jews. They also rejected Sabbath and dietary regulations, celebration of Jewish holidays, and other practices that would have distinguished them from the non-Jewish population. Many adopted these changes as matters of principle and not mere convenience. At a later time, some of the rejected traditional elements would be restored.

In 1885, change was given a theoretical framework when rabbis meeting in Pittsburgh adopted a statement of Reform beliefs and principles. The Pittsburgh Platform spoke of the progressive development of the "God-idea" in Judaism and of Judaism itself as "a progressive religion," meaning that its modern form was bound to be different from its ancient and medieval forms. The rabbis, thinking of evolutionary theory and modern biblical criticism, asserted that scientific research "in the domains of nature and history" was not antagonistic to Jewish history and culture. In the realm of daily living, the talmudic laws "relating to diet, priestly purity, and dress" were not consistent with "modern spiritual elevation." Of the legislation attributed to Moses, they said: "We accept as binding only its moral laws and maintain only such ceremonies as elevate and sanctify our lives, but reject all such as are not adapted to the views and habits of modern civilization."

Thus, in the 1880s, Wise and other reformers could congratulate themselves on the consolidation of the American Reform movement. They had an association of congregations and a platform of principles. They had a small rabbinical college and, by the end of the decade, an association of rabbis. The special circumstances of the German immigration and the American environment had permitted the most modern type of Jewish religion to become the first type to be organized in this country. However, the predominance of Reform among American Jews did not last long.

Opposition to Reform. Although many Jews found Reform attractive, none of these developments occurred without opposition. The ideas of the reforming rabbis split a number of congregations, as with Wise's group in Albany. Sometimes one synagogue became two, one side favoring the new ideas and the other preferring a more traditional style. The old Sefardic synagogues resisted Reform as did a few of the oldest Ashkenazic groups. It is a tribute to Wise's organizing ability that for a decade or so Hebrew Union College and the Union of American Hebrew congregations enjoyed the support even of the more traditionally oriented synagogues, but that fragile alliance was dissolved in the 1880s. The Pittsburgh statement was just too radical to appeal to all American Jews. That, together with certain events at Hebrew Union College, caused conservative elements to secede and open the Jewish Theological Seminary in New York in 1887. However, this disagreement between reformers and conservatives within the predominantly German-descended Jewish population was quickly overshadowed by the arrival of new waves of Jewish immigrants, this time from eastern Europe rather than German-speaking lands. Among them were the most traditionally religious Jews of all, who accepted the term 'Orthodox' to distinguish their religion from other forms of Judaism. As a result of their coming, American Judaism developed into three broad types — Reform, Conservative, and Orthodox — each organized as a "denomination" in the American style. But that result was not evident during the early years of the new immigration.

Orthodoxy Transplanted: The Eastern European Jews

In the mid-nineteenth century, the majority of the world's Jews lived in eastern Europe. Their Ashkenazic ancestors had, for the most part, migrated there between 1290 and 1600, having been banished from England, France, and most of Germany. The rulers of Poland and Lithuania, who together controlled most of eastern Europe in that period, welcomed Jews to assist in developing crafts and commerce in their underdeveloped lands. However, this happy situation deteriorated after a series of revolts and invasions in the seventeenth century. In the following century, Poland and Lithuania were divided up among the Prussian, Austrian, and Russian empires. It is ironic that such a large part of the Jewish population came under the rule of the Russians, who had for centuries barred Jews from Russian soil.

In the nineteenth century, the Tsars of Russia inaugurated various policies designed to "Russify" the Jews by absorbing them into the Russian administrative system and converting the Jews to the Russian Orthodox Church. Among the most harmful efforts were enforced enrollment in Russian-language schools and drafting boys as young as twelve into the army for terms of up to thirty years. Other policies deprived many Jews of employment; disease and starvation were frequent results. Anti-Jewish riots, called "pogroms," were tolerated and sometimes instigated by Russian officials. The situation reached a new degree of desperation after 1881, when the assassination of Tsar Alexander II was falsely but officially blamed on "the Jews." Lynchings, pogroms, expulsions, conscriptions, and bogus trials abounded. One high official said that the intent of Russian policy was to kill a third of the Russian Jews, convert a third, and cause a third to leave.

And so the dam broke. People whose families had resided in the region for four centuries or more began leaving by the thousands for America. There were some eastern European Jews already in the United States, but in 1880 they were a small minority in a Jewish population that originated mainly in the earlier German immigration. But, after 1881, about two million eastern Europeans arrived, swamping the Americanized German Jews. They arrived as the westward movement of the American population was coming to an end and the United States was rapidly increasing its industrial production. Instead of spreading out, as their German predecessors had done, they tended to concentrate in the large industrial cities (half of them in New York) and become industrial workers. They were particularly important in the rapidly expanding clothing industry, in which German Jews were often the employers and eastern Jews the employees.

Culturally, the newcomers were a mixture, ranging from the nearly illiterate to accomplished scholars and artists. A few of them had Russian as their first language, but the great mass of them spoke and read Yiddish as the language of everyday life. Restricted to eastern European Jews, Yiddish was a mixture of German, Hebrew, and Slavic words, structured according to medieval German grammar and written in Hebrew characters. In major cities in the United States, there were newspapers, novels, and plays in Yiddish. Although the holy books — Bible, Talmud, and prayer book — were in Hebrew, which ideally all boys learned to read, the discussion of religious affairs was conducted in Yiddish.

As we approach the religion of the eastern European Jews, it is important to remember that not all of them were religious. Modern ideas had influenced some of the Jews of eastern Europe, where the main results were literary and political rather than religious. There were no efforts to produce a modernized form of Judaism, as in Germany. Instead, the most "modern" Jews simply abandoned religious practice, often in favor of liberal or revolutionary politics. Naturally such people were forced to flee along with the religious Jews. So the eastern European contingent in America included the most secularized Jews as well as the most orthodox. And it is not hard to imagine, in addition, all degrees of day-to-day compromise between the extremes, as dictated by sentiment, habit, or social pressure.

In considering the religious pattern of the eastern European Jews, we should recall the earlier description of traditional Judaism in Germany. The same structure existed in eastern Europe: Bible, Talmud, prayer book, and rabbi-as-teacher (rather than as "minister"). But in eastern Europe, there was a stricter standard of observance and a more evident emotional fervor. The study of the holy books was raised virtually to the level of ritual, at the same time providing the principal recreation of a large segment of the male population. Even the least learned could read the prayer book; that is, if they needed to do so, for the majority of them knew most of the prayers by heart, along with the proper melodies for chanting them. Thus, in any minyan of Orthodox easterners, most of the men were capable of leading the congregation.

This level of observance and learning was maintained by the Jewish educational system, which was widely accessible for boys and very restricted for girls. The aim of the system was to teach pupils to read the holy books in Hebrew. The highest schools were the yeshivas, which provided the brightest boys — beginning in their early teens — with advanced training in talmudic interpretation. Those who completed the course were certified as rabbis. Even those who left early to enter other occupations set a remarkable standard of religious knowledge and conformity among the people.

The main unit of Jewish life in eastern Europe was not the synagogue but the "community." Jews and their Christian overlords agreed (for different reasons) that Jews should be organized as a "nation within a nation." Each community (a village or other residential area) was a unit of the Jewish people. Its leading citizens took turns on the community council (*kahal*), which was responsible for all aspects of community welfare, including commerce, education, worship, poor-relief, and burial. Among other duties, the council maintained the synagogue (the house of prayer), the ritual bath, and other facilities related to worship and ritual purity. Thus, the rabbi was an employee not of the synagogue but of the community, hired as principal educator, talmudic counselor, and local judge. Indeed, the synagogue had no independent organization apart from the community.

For a number of reasons, this pattern of total community organizations did not take root in the United States. Cities were not hospitable places for communal life; they tended to dissolve traditional ties. Furthermore, the American system did not lend any authority to the concept of a nation within a nation. No group of Jewish leaders could enforce its decisions over other Jews. All Jewish affiliations were strictly voluntary. In that case, what alternative form of organization was available? Earlier groups of Jews in the United States had developed a pattern. As we have seen, their principal organization was the religious congregation — the synagogue or temple — similar to the congregations of the Protestant majority. The eastern Europeans followed the American pattern. They organized two thousand new synagogues before 1920.

Many of these synagogues were very small, limited to the survivors of a single village; others were much larger.

As with urban blacks a little later, these Jews often worshiped in storefronts and basements. When they had the means, they attempted to carry out some of the other functions of the old communities, but the costs of certain vital services — cemeteries, burial funds, relief funds, and other forms of mutual assistance — were too high for a single synagogue. The solution was for Jews from several congregations to band together in charitable associations.

In a similar fashion, many Orthodox Jews tried to solve the problem of re-establishing traditional schools. At the elementary level, some teachers set up one-room schools in crowded apartments and tried to teach the Bible and prayer book to young children. The larger (and better) schools were supported by charitable associations rather than by a single teacher or congregation. In 1896, the Rabbi Isaac Elchanan Theological Seminary was established, becoming the first yeshiva in America. It eventually expanded to become Yeshiva University. Meanwhile most of the education of Jewish children was taking place in the public schools, with the Jewish schools usually meeting outside of public school hours. For a variety of reasons, the majority of children were untouched by these institutions. In 1910, only about a fifth of the Jewish school-age children in New York were receiving any form of Jewish education.

In the absence of the institutional structure of eastern Europe, Orthodox leaders began organizing religious associations in the American manner. In 1898, the Union of Orthodox Jewish Congregations was formed, followed by the Union of Orthodox Rabbis four years later. In 1930, English-speaking Orthodox rabbis formed the Rabbinical Council of America. Owing to many divisions among Orthodox Jews, the majority of Orthodox synagogues and rabbis remained outside these groups.

Conservative Judaism, A Middle Way

We saw earlier the slender beginnings of Conservative Judaism when the Jewish Theological Seminary opened in New York in 1887, sponsored by the few old Sefardic congregations and the anti-Reform element among the Germans. These people, though opposed to Reform, were also unsympathetic with the Orthodoxy of the eastern Europeans, which they regarded as noisy, nitpicking, and oblivious to the American environment.

At the turn of the century some of these original conservatives decided to strengthen Jewish Theological Seminary by drawing students from among the sons of eastern European immigrants. Many of these young men, some with excellent Orthodox education, were departing from Orthodox religion. They did not even consider Reform as an option because of a variety of social and religious barriers. (However, many of the following generation, the grandchildren of immigrants, did choose Reform.) A third option was required, starting with a type of rabbinical training that combined traditional studies in Bible and Talmud with modern studies in history and philosophy. With this in mind, the supporters of Jewish Theological Seminary raised a large fund to revitalize the institution. In 1902, they brought from England the world-famous scholar, Solomon Schechter (1850-1915), to be the new president. He gathered a distinguished faculty, who combined, as he did, the traditional talmudic education with studies in the German universities. The seminary began producing rabbis steeped in traditional Judaism who could also understand and appreciate modern western scholarship.

The alumni of the Seminary had already formed the Rabbinical Assembly of America in 1901. The congregations they served began to call themselves Conservative, distinguished from both Orthodox and Reform. In 1913, Schechter founded the United Synagogue of America, an association of Conservative synagogues. Upon Schechter's death in 1915, Cyrus Adler (1863-1940) became president of the United Synagogue and the Seminary. The Conservative movement grew considerably between the world wars, temporarily surpassing the number of Reform members. After World War II, both Conservativism and Reform grew at the expense of Orthodoxy. Now each of the three denominations or types of Judaism claims about one-third of the religiously affiliated Jews in this country.

Conservative Jews dislike having their religion described as a compromise between two other forms of Judaism. In fact, they sometimes think of themselves as "authentic American Judaism," adapting the ancient tradition to a radically new environment. In worship, most Conservative congregations accepted such innovations as family seating, mixed choirs, and organ music. But the prayers were in Hebrew and were often led by a professional cantor. The Conservative prayer book, when it was issued in 1946, differed only slightly from the Orthodox prayer book. This effort to maintain traditional worship among thoroughly Americanized Jews has been one of the hallmarks of Conservative Judaism.

The movement has also encouraged observance of Sabbath regulations, dietary laws, and other elements of talmudic legislation. However, Conservative practice in these matters has not been uniform. The rabbis have tended to be thoroughly observant, much like the Orthodox, while their congregations have been less so, sometimes much less so. Despite such internal tensions, Conservative Judaism exerts a continuing and perhaps growing attraction upon American Jews.

Jews Without Judaism: Religion and Ethnicity

From the beginning of mass immigration, a large number of American Jews have been entirely separate from synagogues and religious activities. Yet they thought of themselves as Jews and were usually regarded as such by other Jews. Although some Jews believed that one could not be a Jew without being religious, most Jews agreed that they were an ethnic group — a "nationality" or a "people" — characterized by other features in addition to a distinctive religion.

It is easier to see Jews as an ethnic group by looking at the European situation before urbanization and mass emigration. Jews were treated as a "nation" with the status of resident aliens. They had no objection to this arrangement, for they believed they were a nation exiled from their homeland. They wanted to govern themselves by talmudic law. They did not want to be integrated into the general citizenry and stop living as Jews. Everyone within the Jewish communities observed, more or less, the traditional Jewish religion. To be an ethnic Jew meant being also a religious Jew, just as to be an Italian once meant being a Catholic. As time went on, it became possible for Jews who changed their minds about religion to cease all or part of the practice of religion. As long as they did not become Christians, they were still viewed as Jews (though as ignorant and apostate Jews) by the religious members of the community. Language, diet, occupation, and other characteristics identified them as Jews. Above all, they were Jewish by association with and concern for other Jews and by their desire to be Jews.

As we saw earlier, these non-religious Jews came to America. Here their numbers were increased, because circumstances allowed an easier departure from Jewish religion. In the late 1930s, only a little more than a quarter of American Jews were affiliated with synagogues or temples. Thus the word "Jew" means either a member of an ethnic group (analogous to "Italian" or "German") or a member of a religious group (analagous to "Christian") or both. The same double meaning haunts the word "Jewish." By contrast "Judaism" and "Judaic" are used to refer specifically to Jewish religion, while "Jewishness" denotes the non-religious or not-necessarily-religious features of Jewish life. Expressions of Jewishness in this country have included literature, drama, journalism, political activity, schools, youth camps, and cultural centers. Some Jews believed, especially in the 1920s and 1930s, that Judaism would decline even further and that the Jewish people would survive through the network of non-religious institutions. That prediction was incorrect, because Judaism has proved to be more resilient than it appeared to be forty years ago.

Religion and ethnicity have intertwined in many ways, particularly when Jews are under pressure. Let us look at three developments between the world wars — Jewish defense against anti-Semitism, the Zionist movement, and certain changes in Reform Judaism — as examples of how ethnic concerns reached across the line between religious and non-religious Jews.

Anti-Semitism and Jewish Defense. The virulent anti-Semitism of Christian Europe was not transferred to North America in colonial times. In the nineteenth century, American nativists concentrated their hostility mainly on the larger Catholic minority. With the appearance of a larger number of Jews in the 1880s, Jews began to be mentioned along with Catholic nationalities in the nativist propaganda. Well-to-do Jews found themselves barred from fashionable resorts, clubs, and schools. "Christians Only" notices began to appear in job advertisements. Agrarian politicians began blaming "Jewish money power" for the farmer's ills. In 1915, Leo Frank, a young Jew, was lynched after being falsely convicted of murdering a girl in Atlanta, Georgia. In this episode, all the racial falsehoods about black lust and cruelty were applied to Jews. Indeed, the pseudo-scientific racial theory that placed Jews and blacks together at the bottom of the "racial" scale was widely believed in the United States (as well as in Europe) from this time on.

After World War I, the notion of the "Jewish world conspiracy" spread across the country. In Europe, the idea was most potently expressed in a Russian anti-Semitic forgery called *The Protocols of The Elders of Zion,* which purported to be records of Jewish leaders in the process of taking over the nations of the world. In the period 1920-1927, industrialist Henry Ford published material from the *Protocols* in the *Dearborn Independent,* also publishing the articles in a series of volumes he entitled *The*

International Jew.

In the face of such slander and assault, Jews organized for defense. Three organizations were particularly noted for effective opposition to anti-Semitism. The first was the American Jewish Committee, founded in 1906 to aid victims of Russian pogroms, and then later adding domestic defense to its agenda. In 1927, the Committee's president, Louis Marshall, obtained from Henry Ford a retraction of the anti-Jewish libels in his publications, along with an apology for printing them. The second major defense organization was the Anti-Defamation League, founded in 1913 as an arm of a much older Jewish fraternal organization, B'nai B'rith. The ADL undertook a broad program of public education in an effort to answer anti-Jewish charges. The American Jewish Congress was founded in 1919 and reconstituted in 1922. Vigorous in its attack on racism and superpatriotism, the Congress was also related to the Zionist movement.

In the 1930s, anti-Semitism in Europe moved toward a climax of atrocity. Adolf Hitler used racial and world conspiracy theories to gain popular support, and in 1933, the control of the German government. His Nazi party progressed from defamation to discrimination to deportation of Jews, all seasoned with official and semiofficial violence. In 1942, the "final solution" was instituted, as certain prison camps were converted into permanent extermination centers. By the summer of 1945, 90 percent of Europe's Jews, one-third of the world Jewish population, were dead. Meanwhile, American anti-Semitism also reached new heights during the 1930s. The Great Depression led people to look for simple answers to hard questions. Some Americans found the answer in "Jewish world domination," "Jewish money power," "Jewish Communism," or a combination of the three together. Some prominent anti-Semites were well-known Protestant and Catholic clergymen. Others formed fascistic, semi-military organizations, such as the Silver Shirts. The German-American Bund was also a source of anti-Jewish publicity.

Defamation at home and slaughter abroad had the effect of drawing American Jews together. We have seen how circumstances led the Jewish population along many paths of development, religious and non-religious. But Jewish Americans perceived that the anti-Semitic attack was as broad as the label "Jew"; accordingly, the defense had to be based just as broadly. Refugee aid, anti-defamation work, and other aspects of the work drew the support of all segments of the Jewish population. In particular, the movement called Zionism gained new support because of anti-Jewish activity.

Zionism in the United States. Mount Zion is the rocky prominence on which the oldest part of the city of Jerusalem is situated. In ancient times, it was the site of the capital and central Temple of the Israelite kingdom. Therefore, the word "Zion" has been used metaphorically since biblical times to refer to Jerusalem and by extension to the whole ancient homeland: Palestine or Eretz Israel (Land of Israel). All but a few Jews were forced to leave Palestine by the fourth century, but Jews continued to express the expectation that God would intervene to allow a general return to Eretz Israel. Strictly speaking, Zionism is the modern political movement to promote Jewish colonization in Palestine and the establishment of a Jewish state there.

Zionism as a political movement came to life in the late nineteenth century under the leadership of Theodore Herzl (1860-1904), an Austrian Jew. His book *Der Judenstaat* (*The Jewish State*, 1896) became the manifesto of the movement. Believing that Jewish statehood was the only solution to resurgent anti-Semitism, Herzl convened the first Zionist Congress in Basel, Switzerland, in 1897. Land was purchased from Arab and Turkish owners, and expeditions of European Jews formed agricultural settlements in Palestine.

These developments brought a mixed response from Jews in the United States. Before World War I, Reform Jews generally opposed Zionism, Conservatives tended to favor it, and the Orthodox were split over the issue as were the non-religious Jews. During the First World War, the British government declared support for a Jewish "national home" in Palestine (Balfour Declaration, 1917). This hopeful sign resulted in increased support from American Jews. The American Jewish Congress, the Jewish National Fund, the woman's association Hadassah, and other Zionist political and fund-raising organizations became active after the war. The rise of Hitlerism and the emigration of persecuted Jews to Palestine in the thirties and forties escalated American Zionism to a mass movement. Most Jews saw Eretz Israel as a land of refuge that would save Jewish lives, especially as they learned of the horrors of the death camps in the 1940s. The events of 1947 and 1948 ended one chapter in Zionist history and began another: the UN partitioning of Palestine, the end of British rule there, and the declaration and successful defense of the republic of Israel.

The overwhelming majority of Jews saw Zionism as an ethnic defense strategy of such importance that religious issues had to be laid aside. Thus, an essentially non-religious movement drew the support of religious Jews because they saw themselves as part of a larger body, the

Jewish people. For Reform Jews especially this viewpoint required a big change from an earlier belief. The original Reform position, stated in the Pittsburgh Platform of 1885, was that Jews were "no longer a nation but a religious community." Accordingly, the Reform rabbis, in 1897, unanimously rejected the call of the Zionist Congress to work for the restoration of a Jewish state in Palestine. In the 1930s, however, this position changed, partly because of the large influx of eastern-descended Jews into Reform temples and partly because of the pressure of anti-Semitism at home and abroad. In 1937, the Columbus Declaration, a new statement of principles replacing the Pittsburgh Platform, spoke of the obligation to help "in the rehabilitation of Palestine .... as a Jewish homeland." Thus, Reform Jews, who originally rejected the perpetuation of Jewish ethnicity in America, came to support the idea of a national home and, in other ways, to express their ties to Jews beyond the realm of "religion only."

Jews and Judaism Since Midcentury

As stated in previous chapters, the biggest religious news in the fifteen years following World War II was the religious revival, marked by burgeoning membership rolls, unprecedented financial support, and the construction of thousands of new religious buildings. Judaism was proportionally more affected by these trends than other religions. By 1960, synagogue membership had risen to about fifty percent of self-identified Jews, about double the pre-war level.

The reasons for this resurgence of religious institutions are hard to pin down, even though a great deal has been written about the phenomenon. As a general condition, applying to the bulk of the American population, one should not forget the prosperity of the period. In a half-century, the business or professional office had replaced the factory and sweatshop as the typical Jewish workplace, which meant that Jews could afford the costs of rejuvenated institutional life. Furthermore, Jews newly arrived in the middle class were adopting the norms of other middle class Americans, for whom religious activity was an important feature of family and community life. Also, as Jews drew further away in time from the immigrant generation, they placed higher value on the traditions of their grandparents and great-grandparents. This evaluation was enhanced by the European catastrophe, after which American Jews felt a need to reaffirm their solidarity with those who had been massacred. Thus, religious affiliation served the purpose of renewed ethnic loyalty.

The resurgence of synagogues was also related to the concerns of young parents recently moved to the suburbs, where Jewish families found themselves with many Christian neighbors. They felt the need to assure their children the means to understand their Jewish heritage and to maintain Jewish identity. The most accessible way to accomplish this was to join a congregation and support its educational program.

In addition to these factors connected with group identity and family life, it is reasonable to suppose that Jews also joined synagogues and attended services for internal and specifically religious motives. They were searching for meaning and order in their lives and in the world. One indicator of this sort of motive was the increased sales of books on Jewish themes, such as the many works of Abraham Joshua Heschel, who wrote of universal human concerns while seeking to lead modern Jews to a deeper appreciation of their religious tradition.

Along with increased synagogue affiliation, Zionism has continued to be a major expression of Jewish consciousness for people outside and inside the synagogues. American Jews contribute many millions of dollars to Israel each year, although contributions are at a reduced level from the peak year of 1948, the year of Israel's independence. The reduction has been largely due to the needs of synagogues and charitable institutions at home. Nevertheless, the majority of Jews find the existence of Israel important to their own inner sense of well-being. When Israel has been at war, as in 1956, 1967, and 1973, Jewish feeling has been noticeably solidified. It is significant that Israel's Independence Day became a religious-ethnic holiday for American Jews, much like the ancient festivals of Purim and Hanukah. However, relations between Israelis and American Jews are not always smooth. The matter of emigration is a smoldering issue. When American Jews speak of the Jewish national home, they normally do not mean a home for themselves. Very few American Jews have become citizens of Israel, a fact that irritates some Israelis, who feel that the skills possessed by American Jews are even more important to Israel's future than American dollars. Conversely the policies of Israel's government do not always meet with the approval of Jews in this country. It must be added that the existence of Israeli nationality as an option has complicated older notions of Jewish ethnicity.

The Three Varieties of Judaism: Reform, Conservatism, Orthodoxy. In the postwar period and down to the present time, Judaism has continued to be expressed in three principal types. Despite great differences among them, they can all be seen as adaptations and variations of the traditional religion of the ancient rabbis. Each of the three serves the needs of a segment of the Jewish population, and each appears to have a future in the American religious scene.

Reform Judaism has been characterized by a reaffirming of certain traditional elements in worship and celebration. Jewish holidays are observed in schools, synagogues, and homes of the Reform sector. Some of the congregational prayers have been restored to the Hebrew language. The teaching of Hebrew has become an objective of some Reform education, partly to facilitate worship in Hebrew and partly because of the connection with the state of Israel, where Hebrew is the mother tongue. Hebrew Union College and Jewish Institute of Religion, the rabbinical training facilities of the Reform movement, maintain a branch in Israel, partly in order to assure familiarity with Hebrew among the new generation of rabbis. At the same time, a certain number of Orthodox-educated men have become Reform rabbis. Some temples are eager to be served by a rabbi who can guarantee, so to speak, an authentic link with the past, including the talmudic tradition.

Conservative Judaism has continued as a satisfying position for Jews moving from both left and right. Children of Reform and Orthodox parents often choose Conservative congregations. Like other types of Jews, the Conservatives are apt to feel that their way represents what is best in Judaism. Their success since World War II suggests that a large number of Jews agree with the Conservative way. Yet the nature of the movement has still not been clearly defined, because the defining authority is not clearly constituted. The Rabbinical Assembly tends to be traditional in its positions, while the United Synagogue, consisting of representatives from the congregations, is inclined to be tolerant of departures from traditional law. Lay people complain that the rabbis are slow to accommodate the genuine problems of conscientious observance in a modern society. In recent years, however, the rabbis have responded on certain issues. For instance, the law forbids traveling on the Sabbath. In suburban congregations, this restriction would leave Sabbath services largely unattended, so the Assembly has reluctantly modified it. On many other issues, however, people feel that they are left to choose between impossible observance and undesirable non-observance. In some cases, there is no perceptible difference between a

Conservative Jew and a Reform Jew in matters of diet, Sabbath observance, and other traditional behavior.

A person unfamiliar with Jewish life would suppose that the Orthodox are the most unified of all Judaic types, because of their proclaimed commitment to the traditional sources of Jewish religion. However, many points of tradition are subject to disagreement, and those who are the strictest adherents of the talmudic way are the ones who disagree the most. This is partially owing to local variations and religious disputes carried over from Europe. In addition, the very strict Orthodox movement called Hasidism is divided by strong loyalties to particular leaders. Then there is the so-called Modern Orthodoxy associated with Yeshiva University. This is not accepted by the groups, such as the Hasidic people, who value Yiddish as a semisacred language of religious discussion. Despite these sharp divisions within Orthodoxy, the movement as a whole is displaying a power and appeal that few would have predicted a half-century ago. A minority of the young from Reform and Conservative and non-religious homes are choosing to become Orthodox. At the same time, some Orthodox groups have undertaken vigorous and imaginative missionary efforts. Often mentioned in this regard are the Lubavitcher Hasidim under their venerable rebbe Menachem Schneerson. Schneerson and some of his followers fled from the Nazis in 1940 and established a new Lubavitcher center in Brooklyn, New York. Now they have branches in several cities, where they are engaged in persuading Jews of other viewpoints to adopt Orthodox practices. Their facilities and methods include not only houses of prayer and kosher restaurants but also sound trucks and street displays.

From this brief description it appears that all sectors of Judaism are related to the Jewish tradition, though in different ways; and all have been obliged to adapt creatively to the world of modern America. America has challenged the Jewish people, as much by its hospitality as by its hostility. When Jews arrived in this country, their problem was how to fit in, how to be American though Jewish. Although some may have doubts, most Jews will agree that that problem has been solved. Now the concern of thoughtful Jews is how to be Jewish though American.

Selected People and Events

1492 Jews expelled from Spain, and, four years later, from Portugal.

1648 Cossack uprising in the Ukraine; many Jews killed; beginning of a long period of worsening conditions for eastern European Jews, accompanied by partial migration back to western Europe.

1654 A group of Portuguese-speaking Jews arrived in New Amsterdam (soon to become New York); first Jews in North America.

1763 Dedication of the synagogue in Newport, Rhode Island, the only eighteenth-century North American synagogue building still in existence.

1802 Establishment of the first congregation in North America using Ashkenazic, rather than Sefardic, ritual (Philadelphia).

1836 First mass movement of Jews to the United States began in Bavaria.

1843 Isaac Leeser (1806-1868), Hazzan (cantor) and principal leader of the old Sefardic synagogue in Philadelphia, founded the *Occident and Jewish Advocate*, the first American Jewish newspaper and a strong supporter of conservative tendencies in American Judaism.

1854 Isaac Meyer Wise (1819-1900) founded the *American Israelite* in Cincinnati in support of Reform Judaism against Lesser's *Occident.*

1873 Founding of the Union of American Hebrew Congregations, the first association of Jewish congregations in America; became identified with Reform, as distinguished from more traditional types of American Judaism.

1875 Founding of Hebrew Union College in Cincinnati, the first viable Jewish institution of higher learning in America; became identified with Reform.

1881 Beginning of a mass movement of Jews from eastern Europe as a result of pogroms and anti-Jewish laws following the assassination of Tsar Alexander II of Russia.

1885 An important statement of Reform principles and beliefs was adopted by rabbis meeting in Pittsburgh.

1898 Founding of the Union of Orthodox Jewish Congregations.

1887 Opening of the Jewish Theological Seminary in New York, representing what came to be called Conservative Judaism.

1894 Publication of the Union Prayer Book of Reform rabbis.

1896 Founding in New York of the Rabbi Isaac Elchanan Theological Seminary, an Orthodox yeshiva (rabbinical academy) in the eastern European educational tradition; developed into the present-day Yeshiva University.

1897 The first Zionist Congress met in Basel, Switzerland; Reform rabbis in the United States unanimously condemned Zionism.

1912 Henrietta Szold founded Hadassah, The Women's Zionist Organization of America, thus mobilizing Jewish women for the Zionist cause.

1913 Solomon Schechter founded the United Synagogue of America, an association of Conservative congregations.

1925 Quota system reduced eastern European migration to a trickle.

1933 Adolf Hitler took power; beginning of the persecution and migration of German Jews.

1942 American Zionists adopt the Biltmore Platform calling for a Jewish state in Palestine; overwhelming majority of Reform rabbis supported Zionism (compare 1897).

1944 American Jews become aware of the extent of the catastrophe in Europe; 90 percent of European Jews dead by the summer of 1945.

1948 Declaration of a Jewish state in Palestine, followed by Israel's defense of its independence against an alliance of Arab nations.

1951 Increased interest in Jewish religious thought was indicated by the publication of Abraham Joshua Heschel's *Man Is Not Alone* and Will Herberg's *Judaism for Modern Man.*

1962 Synagogue construction and membership reached a plateau and began declining after several years of rapid growth.

1967 Israel's Six-Day War produced "an unexpected and overwhelming reaction among American Jews" (Glazer, 198), including a renewed feeling of Jewish identity and a deterioration of Jewish-Christian dialogue.

1976 Enrollment in full-time Jewish day schools (mostly Orthodox) rose to 82,000, a 36 percent increase in ten years.

SUGGESTIONS FOR FURTHER STUDY

1. General Works

Ahlstrom, Sydney E., *A Religious History of the American People.* New Haven: Yale University Press, 1972. The fullest and most recent general account. Fine narrative supplemented by helpful notes and bibliography.

Carroll, Jackson W., Johnson, Douglas W., and Marty, Martin E. *Religion in America, 1950 to the Present.* San Francisco: Harper and Row, 1979. Articles, maps, and statistical tables.

Gaustad, Edwin Scott. *Historical Atlas of Religion in America.* Rev. ed. New York: Harper and Row, 1976.

Hudson, Winthrop S. *Religion in America: An Historical Account of the Development of American Religious Life.* 2nd ed. New York: Charles Scribner's Sons, 1973. Good comprehensive narrative.

Melton, J. Gordon. *A Directory of Religious Bodies in the United States.* New York: Garland Publishing, 1977. Classifies and lists primary religious groups.

Melton, J. Gordon. *The Encyclopedia of American Religions.* 2 vols. Wilmington, N.C.: McGrath Publishing Co., 1978. Especially helpful for small groups; good system of classification.

Smith, H. Shelton, Handy, Robert T., and Loetscher, Lefferts A. *American Christianity: An Historical Interpretation with Representative Documents.* 2 vols. New York: Charles Scribner's Sons, 1960-1963. Sources combined with good narrative.

2. Indian Religion

Berkhofer, Robert F., Jr. *Salvation and the Savage: An Analysis of Protestant Missions and American Indian Response, 1787-1862.* New York: Atheneum, 1972; orig. pub. 1965. Shows conflict between Indian and white cultures.

Black Elk. *Black Elk Speaks, Being the Life Story of a Holy Man of the Oglala Sioux.* As told through John G. Neihardt. New York: Pocket Books, 1972. Autobiography showing an Indian world view.

Black Elk. *The Sacred Pipe: Black Elk's Account of the Seven Rites of the Oglala Sioux.* Rec. and edit. by Joseph Epes Brown. Baltimore: Penguin Books, 1971; orig. pub., 1953.

McNickle, D'Arcy. *They Came Here First: The Epic of the American Indian.* Rev. ed. New York: Harper and Row, 1975.

Marriott, Alice, and Rachlin, Carol K. *American Epic: The Story of the American Indian.* New York: New American Library, 1969.

Marriott, Alice, and Rachlin, Carol K. *American Indian Mythology.* New York: New American Library, 1968. Includes recent myths.

Marriott, Alice, and Rachlin, Carol K. *Peyote.* New York: Thomas Y. Crowell Co., 1971. History and status of the peyote movement.

Slotkin, J.S. "The Peyote Way," in Tedlock, *Teachings from the American Earth.* Description and interpretation by an anthropologist-believer.

Tedlock, Dennis, and Tedlock, Barbara, eds. *Teachings from the American Earth: Indian Religion and Philosophy.* New York: Liveright, 1975.

Underhill, Ruth. *Red Man's Religion: Beliefs and Practices of the Indians North of Mexico.* Chicago: University of Chicago Press, 1965. Survey of regions and topics.

3. White Protestantism

Anderson, Charles H. *White Protestant Americans: From National Origins to Religious*

Group. Englewood Cliffs, N.J.: Prentice-Hall, Inc., 1970. History of ethnic groups.

Bailey, Kenneth K. *Southern White Protestantism in the Twentieth Century.* New York: Harper and Row, 1964.

Cross, Whitney R. *The Burned-Over District: The Social and Intellectual History of Enthusiastic Religion in Western New York, 1800-1850.* Ithaca, N.Y.: Cornell University Press, 1950.

Furniss, Norman K. *The Fundamentalist Controversy, 1918-1931.* New Haven: Yale University Press, 1954. The split between liberals and conservatives.

Marty, Martin E. *Righteous Empire: The Protestant Experience in America.* New York: Dial Press, 1970. General account beginning with the Revolution.

Mathews, Donald G. *Religion in the Old South.* Chicago: University of Chicago Press, 1977. Includes both black and white religion, 1750-1860.

May, Henry F. *Protestant Churches and Industrial America.* New York: Harper and Row, 1949. Covers 1828-1895.

Winslow, Ola Elizabeth. *Meetinghouse Hill, 1630-1783.* New York: W.W. Norton & Co., 1972; orig. pub. 1952. Social history of Puritan churches.

4. Black Religion

Barrett, Leonard E. *Soul-Force: African Heritage in Afro-American Religion.* Garden City, N.Y.: Anchor Press/Doubleday, 1974.

Cone, James H. *Black Theology and Black Power.* New York: Seabury Press, 1969. Important work in the modern Black Theology movement.

Cone, James H. *The Spirituals and the Blues: An Interpretation.* New York: Seabury Press, 1972.

DuBois, W.E. Burghardt. *The Souls of Black Folk.* New York: Fawcett World Library, 1961; orig. pub. 1903. Classic essays on black life and religion.

Levine, Lawrence W. *Black Culture and Black Consciousness: Afro-American Folk Thought from Slavery to Freedom.* Oxford: Oxford University Press, 1977. Includes accounts of folk beliefs, spirituals, and gospel music.

Meier, August, and Rudwick, Elliott. *From Plantation to Ghetto.* 3rd ed. New York: Hill and Wang, 1976. General history of blacks in the U.S.

Raboteau, Albert J. *Slave Religion: The "Invisible Institution" in the Antebellum South.* New York: Oxford University Press, 1978. Includes African background.

Scherer, Lester B. *Slavery and the Churches in Early America, 1619-1819.* Grand Rapids, Mich.: William B. Eerdmans Publishing Co., 1975. Background for the early development of black religion.

Sobel, Mechal. *Trabelin' On: The Slave Journey to an Afro-Baptist Faith.* Westport, Conn.: Greenwood Press, 1979. Includes a catalog of early black Baptist churches.

Synan, Vinson. *The Holiness-Pentecostal Movement.* Grand Rapids, Mich.: William B. Eerdmans Publishing Co., 1971. Includes developments among whites as well as blacks.

Washington, James M. "The Origins and Emergence of Black Baptist Separatism, 1863-1897." Ph.D. dissertation. Yale University, 1979.

5. Roman Catholicism

Abell, Aaron I. *American Catholicism and Social Action: A Search for Social Justice, 1865-1950.* Garden City, N.Y.: Hanover House, 1960.

Callahan, Daniel. *The Mind of the Catholic Layman.* New York: Charles Scribner's Sons, 1963.

Cross, Robert D. *The Emergence of Liberal Catholicism in America.* Cambridge, Mass.: Harvard University Press, 1967 (c. 1958). Late nineteenth century.

Dolan, Jay P. *Catholic Revivalism: The American Experience, 1830-1900.* Notre Dame, Ind.: University of Notre Dame Press, 1978. Parish missions.

Dolan, Jay P. *The Immigrant Church: New York's Irish and German Catholics, 1815-1865.* Baltimore: Johns Hopkins University Press, 1975.

Ellis, John Tracy. *American Catholicism.* 2nd ed. Chicago: University of Chicago Press, 1969. The standard one-volume history.

Greeley, Andrew M. *The Catholic Experience.* Garden City, N.Y.: Doubleday & Co., 1969. Leaders and issues from John Carroll to John Kennedy.

McAvoy, Thomas T. *The Formation of the American Catholic Minority.* Philadelphia: Fortress Press, 1967.

Wakin, Edward, and Scheuer, Joseph F. *The De-Romanization of the American Catholic Church.* New York: MacMillan Co., 1966.

6. Judaism

Blau, Joseph L. *Judaism in America: From Curiosity to Third Faith.* Chicago: University of Chicago Press, 1976. General account.

Blau, Joseph L. *Modern Varieties of Judaism.* New York: Columbia University Press, 1966.

Howe, Irving. *World of Our Fathers.* New York: Simon and Schuster, 1977. Eastern European Jews in the nineteenth and twentieth centuries in the U.S.

Glazer, Nathan. *American Judaism.* 2nd ed. Chicago: University of Chicago, 1972. Standard one-volume history.

Neusner, Jacob. *American Judaism: Adventure in Modernity.* Englewood Cliffs, N.J.: Prentice-Hall, Inc., 1972. An interpretation of the nature of American Judaism.

Neusner, Jacob, ed. *Understanding American Judaism: Toward A Description of a Modern Religion.* 2 vols. New York: Ktav Publishing House and Anti-Defamation League of B'nai B'rith, 1975. Selected articles.

Rischin, Moses. *The Promised City: New York's Jews, 1870-1914.* New York: Corinth Books, 1964.

Sklare, Marshall. *Conservative Judaism: An American Religious Movement.* Glencoe, Ill.: Free Press, 1955. Sociological study.

INDEX